"Daniel Harris has w
simple but profoun
something we do in spasms, ...
sort emerges. In so doing, we have reduced prayer to what is
essentially a fire alarm box. It just sits there unused except in
an emergency. Then we pull the handle. This is not a book
about praying longer, or praying more earnestly, or praying
more loudly. Rather, it is a challenge to introduce the rhythm
of prayer into one's life so that one does indeed "Live
Prayerfully." Through silent prayer, the written prayers of
others and one's own prayers, plus Scripture and hymnody,
we enter the presence of the Holy One at four critical times of
any twenty-four hour period: in the morning, at midday, in the
early evening, and before one retires for the day. My wife and I
have been following this suggestion, and both of us too have
been learning and discovering more of how to live prayerfully.
I invite you to join us in this adventure."

Victor P. Hamilton, retired professor of Bible and Theology,
Asbury University and author of the two-volume commentary,
The Book of Genesis

"An accessible and insightful book on how to pray—so that
our lives become rooted in God's presence all of the time. I
found the daily guides to prayer and additional resources for
further praying especially helpful. Harris' personal and
humble approach to the crucial discipline of prayer make this
book something that seasoned pray-ers as well as those
without much 'prayer practice' can benefit from."

Joannah Sadler, managing editor, *Conversations Journal*

"It was a pleasure to read this book and to now recommend it
for those who simply want to get on with praying and
developing an authentic friendship with God."

Sibyl Towner, spiritual director, co-founder of OneLifeMaps,
and co-director of The Springs Retreat Center, Indiana

"Prayerful living entails both intentionality and spontaneity. Daniel Harris' work shows what such a combination looks like in concrete fashion! Here's a no-frills piece that brings the cookie jar of prayer into the lower shelf—accessible, relatable, and doable. Harris's memorable three-point outline captures succinctly the essence of how to live prayerfully while his corresponding guides demonstrate well its practical outworking. Definitely a helpful tool for beginners and practitioners alike!"

Wil Hernandez, spiritual director, retreat leader, and author of a trilogy on Henri Nouwen

"*Live Prayerfully* offers a refreshingly simple (though not easy!) way to pray for those who desire to live in the immediacy of relationship with God. Though steeped in the spiritual writings of the past, the book breathes with the life and experience of its author, Daniel Harris. He avoids focusing on replication of technique while inviting readers to pray in a way that affects the way ordinary people live with God the rest of their day. Harris' conversational tone in the first half of the book is complemented nicely by the rich resources for praying he provides in the second half. I highly recommend *Live Prayerfully!*"

Clair Allen Budd, chair, Dept. of Christian Studies and Philosophy, Asbury University

"In *Live Prayerfully*, Daniel Harris reminds us that prayer is not meant to be complicated but rather simple communication with our Father. Just as God has never created anyone exactly like you, with your unique personality, the way you talk to God and the way He communicates and relates to you is unique as well. How freeing to know that I don't have to mimic someone else's prayer life."

Kendon Wheeler, president, New Life Advance International

"*Live Prayerfully* provides a fresh and creative three part process of prayer that includes praying with other people's words, praying without words, and praying with your own words. The book also gives practical ways to incorporate this process into your daily prayer life. The book will help Christians develop a daily rhythm of making prayer a natural part of their faith journey. I recommend this book to all who seek to connect with God."

Mark A. Maddix, dean, School of Theology & Christian Ministries, Northwest Nazarene University and co-author of *Discovering Discipleship* and *Spiritual Formation: A Wesleyan Paradigm*

"Daniel Harris inspires us to be the prayerful individuals that God intended for us to be. I am so very grateful for the gift that Daniel has given to us. May we be moved to enter into God's presence in all the wonderful ways that are open to us. Beloved, let us pray...."

Stuart A. Smith, former campus chaplain, Asbury University

"It's in the title: *Live Prayerfully*. If one is going to follow St. Paul's counsel to 'pray without ceasing,' then prayer must move from something that we do to something that we are. A guide for that movement is what Daniel has given us in this book. The ways of praying presented here are ancient practices that expand our capacity for encountering God. But they are also completely practical and presented in an instructive and winsome manner. This book is not just teaching us a way to pray, it is teaching us a way to live...prayerfully."

Robert Pelfrey, Methodist pastor

How Ordinary Lives Become Prayerful

Live
Prayerfully

Daniel Ethan Harris

Salvation
LIFE
BOOKS

SalvationLife Books
www.salvationlife.com/books
E-mail: daniel@salvationlife.com

ISBN-10: 0615715400
ISBN-13: 978-0615715407

Cover design: Roy Migabon: www.roymigabon.co.cc
Cover Image: Jupiterimages/Comstock Images/Getty Images
Author Photograph: Tiffany Harris: www.tharrisphoto.com

In memory of my Dad,
David E. Harris
1944-2010

Please consider offering your thoughts on this book and/or joining in the conversation about it in any or all of these ways:

- Post your comments on the book's page at www.salvationlife.com.
- Offer a review of the book at Amazon.com.
- Post anything you would like to say about the book on Twitter using the hash tag: #LivePrayerfullyBook.

Contents

Foreword

It is always a precious moment when someone who has been your student becomes a teacher and begins to relay what they have learned to others, in their own voice within their own context. It is one of those moments that makes teaching worthwhile! So, I cannot help but feel great pleasure in commending Daniel Harris' work on prayer, knowing that he has been a faithful student—and more importantly, a practice-er—of prayer in our times of shared learning and beyond.

Prayer encompasses all the ways in which we commune and communicate with God for the purpose of cultivating our friendship with him. As Daniel wisely acknowledges, many of us would rather read books on prayer than actually pray so he shares not only his passion for prayer but also the practical approaches that have nourished his own intimacy with God. He divides these approaches into three helpful categories—praying with other people's words, praying without words, and praying with your own words. The second half of the book offers guides to fixed hour prayer which skillfully incorporate all three of these dynamic elements of a prayerful life.

Daniel's winsome invitation to live prayerfully is comprised of down-to-earth illustrations, honesty about his own experiences with prayer, and well-chosen references to the riches of our Christian tradition—often with a bit of gentle humor thrown in. As you read and engage the prayer practices described here, you will discover how ordinary lives can become prayerful, thus causing them to become extraordinary.

Ruth Haley Barton, D.D.
Founder, Transforming Center, and author of
Invitation to Solitude and Silence and *Sacred Rhythms*

Introduction

Searching for Simple and Reliable

My grandfather had a good friend named Alf. They were both cowboys, and they both lived prayerfully. From the time I was a boy, I wanted to know God the way they did. Alf was the type who could tell a great cowboy story about the old days, and I especially liked to listen to him because it wasn't unusual for him to make an off-the-cuff comment about life with God that would stop me in my tracks.

Though I wasn't present to hear him make this particular comment, it made enough of an impact on other friends who heard it that they relayed it to me a year later, after Alf's death. There was a group of men discussing ways that they tried to devote their days to God. Some of them said after getting up in the morning they tried to pray that God would help them to live that day devoted to him, that for that day they could steer clear of temptation, love others well, etc. This is good advice, and we'd all certainly do well to develop such a practice.

At age ninety-one, having lived a lifetime of deep friendship with God, Alf already had the profound respect of everyone in the group that evening. Anyone who knew him knew how prayerful his life had been. So, he surprised everyone when he added his comment to the conversation on how to start a day in devotion to God by admitting he didn't do the good kinds of things they had mentioned. In response to their suggestions of things they prayed to begin the rest of their day, I can picture him looking at the ground with a humble shrug of his shoulders and his grateful smile as he said, "You know, I don't really do that. It just comes natural."

That kind of life in which prayer comes naturally is meant for everyone. Whether we are cowboys, schoolteachers, bankers, engineers, monks, mechanics, pastors, prisoners, or almost anything else, our real lives *can* become thoroughly connected to God.

Many of us sincerely believe the above statement to be true, yet paradoxically also find that prayer doesn't have the place in our own lives that we would like it to have, or even that we think it should have. The aim of this book is to help you to make significant strides toward living as prayerfully as you desire, in the midst of the life you really live.

I believe that part of the obstacle for many of us, standing between the level of connection to God that we have now and how prayerfully we would like to live, is that we have been likely taught one (or possibly two) of the ways to pray discussed in this book, but it is rare for any of us to have learned all three. I believe that practicing these three ways and letting them build on one another can significantly raise the level of prayerfulness in our lives, our churches, our communities, and onward.

Before you think that learning to pray in three ways is going to be something burdensome, I assure you that it is not my approach to add a number of other things having to do with prayer to the already too-full to-do lists that most of us have. Rather, I am convinced that it doesn't necessarily take any more time to pray in all three of the ways we will explore together than it takes to only pray in one of them.

I remember a time as a college student when I wondered what Paul might have meant by saying that we should be "faithful in prayer," as it says in Romans 12:12. Though I didn't think about it long enough to formulate any real answer, my default conclusion was that we should all be praying for *really* long times. At that time in my life, the only one of these three ways of praying that I had learned and was practicing was praying with my own words, so I thought that surely being faithful in prayer would mean that I would spend hours each day praying that way. I signed up for a prayer vigil and took two hours in the middle of the night that no one else would take and spent them praying in the only way I knew how—with my own words. I thought that fulfilling Paul's command would require me to do that kind of thing all the time.

I tried, and it didn't last long. In fact, I've never gotten myself up in the middle of the night to pray for multiple hours since then. When I did it that one time, I was proud of myself for having done so. And for at least a week, I looked back on those couple of hours when I had felt so prayerful in the middle of the night.

More than twelve years have passed since that night, and though I now never attempt to pray for two hours in the middle of the night, I live a more prayerful life now than I did then. I certainly still have times set aside for prayer, but they're usually closer to twenty minutes than they are to two hours. Rather than having to look back at some point earlier in the week or month when I had done something I thought to be prayerful, I now have the sense that I live prayerfully by making regular, short practice of the three ways of praying described in this book. When I do so, I notice that connection to God from those regular shot times spills over into the rest of my days.

Why the Guidance Matters

While I was working on this, a friend read a section and commented, "I can honestly say that I wouldn't normally pick up a book about prayer. To me, it's sort of like exercise; I know I need to do it. I don't feel like I need to know *how* to do it, I just need to do it."

She had a point. Something I've learned about my own personality that can be a weakness is that I can spend far too long collecting all the available information on how to do something, but never get around to actually doing it, because there's always some more information out there. That can't be our approach to prayer. We learn to pray by praying, not by reading about how to pray in books.

To connect to her analogy of exercise: when we aren't praying, or aren't exercising, we can think of both of these activities as things we know we should be doing, and already know how to do, but we just aren't doing. When we aren't praying or exercising, the how-to seems too elementary for us to bother to investigate; to exercise, we could just go out our front doors and start jogging. To start praying we might say something like, "Dear God, please help me _____, please help them _____, please help us _____. Amen." While neither of those approaches are the worst in the world, they also are not the best. That approach to exercise rarely makes an unfit person healthy, and that approach to prayer rarely makes an ordinary life prayerful.

On the other hand, once we begin to attempt exercise or prayer, we find that some good how-to guidance is highly valuable. For example, we find how helpful it is to have a plan, or to learn from those who have already taken the steps we are attempting to take. In exercise, the guidance helps us to avoid injuries and to stick with it when we don't feel like exercising. In prayer, the guidance helps us to shape our prayers in ways we might not think of on our own and to stick with it when we don't feel like praying.

Why We Need Simple and Reliable

Though we may not seek out guidance on exercise or prayer as often as might be helpful for us, we inevitably look for guidance from others in other aspects of our lives. Sometimes we seek it out personally, or perhaps through books and other media. As we do so, you've probably found that occasionally the guidance we get is simple but perhaps not as reliable as we need it to be. For example, it turns out that "an apple a day keeps the doctor away" isn't as true as people would have us believe. I went through a stretch of my life where I ate apples almost every day, usually dipped in mounds of peanut butter, or perhaps together with oatmeal and cinnamon sugar under a pile of ice cream, or (my favorite) in a dessert my wife makes together with gobs of whipped cream and pieces of Snickers bars. I followed the advice to have an apple a day pretty well during those years, but for some reason, while eating those apples in these ways, it was in that same period of time that I went from having recently been a college athlete to hardly being able to even think about running down and back on a basketball court. The doctor visits ensued, despite all the apples I consumed. The advice regarding apples was simple, but not as reliable as I needed it to be.

On the other hand, we've all probably also had experience with advice that is reliable, but not simple enough. If I start having car problems, I can walk into my local auto parts store and locate the thick printed repair guide for my car's make and model. I will have no idea how to do what it says. That does not mean its guidance is unreliable, but it just is not simple enough for me.

Thankfully, though, there is another kind of advice. The best advice we receive in life, the kind that sticks with us for decades and that we make sure to pass on to our children and grandchildren, is that which is both simple and reliable. Dave Ramsey's "Seven Baby Steps" have been helpful to me and millions of others for this reason. Or, I'll never forget sitting with my college pastor as I was preparing to graduate and having the sudden realization that I would no longer be allowed to live in the dorm, eat in the cafeteria and attend classes, but would soon have to find another way to live. As the variety of options seemed rather overwhelming to me, his simple and reliable advice was, "Just make sure you're in God's will today and you won't miss being in it tomorrow." It was simple and reliable; I've never forgotten it and continue to work at shaping my life around it.

From my experience, the need for simple and reliable guidance when we seek to learn to pray is just as needed as in any other part of our lives. Guidance that is described by one end or the other of the simple/reliable spectrum abounds, but guidance that is described by both ends can seem hard to find. So, after having spent quite a bit of time seeking guidance on prayer from sources all across that spectrum, my goal in this book is to pass on some of the most reliable parts of it in simple ways. So, we will take a look at three time-proven ways that ordinary lives have become prayerful:

- Praying With Other People's Words
- Praying Without Words
- Praying With Your Own Words

Prayer Should Make Us Prayerful

In *Coming Home to Your True Self*, Albert Haase relates a conversation with an elderly woman who had been his spiritual director. He asked her, "What's the best way to pray?"

"Actually, the best way to pray is the way that works for you," she replied.

He then asked, "And how am I supposed to find out which way works best for me?"

She said, "By trial and error. Try different techniques until you find one that suits you. The most important thing, Albert, is that our prayers are supposed to *make us prayerful*. That's the critical factor."

"What do you mean?" Albert asked.

"So often, people get in their prayer time and then, once it's over, totally forget God for the rest of the day. They act like they fulfilled their obligation and can now continue with the tasks ahead of them. That's a typical mistake for many of us. Prayer should make us prayerful. In other words, whatever we do during our time of prayer should have an effect on the way we live and act once it's over. Our prayer should make us attentive to the presence of God in the here and now-not just during our scheduled time of prayer but during the rest of the day as well. And so, as we brush our teeth, balance the checkbook or wash the dishes, we have a sense of God's presence as if God were the scent of the freshly cut roses that fills the room." [1]

I love that: *prayer should make us prayerful.* We aren't going to talk about these ways of praying so that any of us can become a master at some way of prayer, to be able to check it off of our to-do list for the day and then go on about the rest of our lives as normal. No, we'll look at these ways of praying so that we can become more prayerful people, who are learning to live as if God was with us right here, and right now.

We'll be reminded of the "prayer should make us prayerful" principle throughout the book, and another recurring theme worth mentioning before we jump in to our first way of praying is: *we don't pray in these ways because of the effect that they might have on us at the time we're doing them.* Rather, we do them at specific times and in specific ways, so that the remainder of our everyday lives can be more open to God, more aware of God's presence with us and in our world. When we view these ways of praying as if they are "on the spot training," then our praying is confined to those specific times that we have set aside for prayer. On the other hand, if we understand that we do these things at specific times and in specific ways because of the effect they can have on the rest of our lives, like "off the spot training," they can become among the most important tools we have for learning to live prayerful lives. In other words, we not only want to *pray* prayerfully, but we want to *live* prayerfully.

Learn to Pray by Praying

I'll finish this Introduction with a confession: even in the days that I've spent writing this, I've had to repent of all the times that I've thought, "Well, maybe I should set aside my normal time of prayer today in order to work on the book about living prayerfully."

It's sad, in a humorous kind of way, but perhaps you can identify with something like my own tendency to prefer to work on this book about prayer, rather than actually pray. I love to read a good book on prayer. I love to go to retreats and conferences and hear great speakers talk about prayer. And then, when it comes time to pray, I can easily find a long list of other things to do.

Yet when we stop to think about it, we know that listening to teaching about prayer or reading books about prayer (or even writing one!) are not sufficient substitutes for finding a real, fulfilling connection to God. We know that the only actual way to learn to pray is by praying. So learning to pray by praying will be the focus of this book. It will give you some tools that have been helpful to millions of other followers of Jesus both today and throughout the centuries past.

Each chapter in Part One of the book will explore one of these three ways to pray, including "For Further

Praying" and "For Further Reading" recommendations for each respective chapter. Part Two of the book is a guide for you to implement the three ways of praying discussed in Part One.

A Life That Makes Prayer Come Naturally

My hope is that this book will be helpful to you in growing toward a prayerful life that "just comes natural," as in Alf's story. There's a paradox in this, though: we think that if something is to come naturally, that means that it doesn't require structure, intentional habits or discipline. Yet the opposite is true. It is structure, intentional habits, and discipline that allow things to flow naturally in us. The talented musician who can sit down at their instrument and "just play anything, whenever they want to" can do so because of all the time they have put into dedicated practice. It is the same with prayer. It was all of Alf's times of intentionally praying that allowed prayer to come so naturally at other times, spilling over from specific times of prayer and, over time, building a prayerful life. I anticipate that if you experiment with intentionally incorporating these three ways of praying into your lifestyle, you will find that living a prayerful life comes very naturally to you as well.

Since the first chapter is on praying with other people's words, I begin by praying these words of St. Paul for you, wherever you may be as you read them:

I pray that, according to the riches of [the Father's] glory, he may grant that you may be strengthened in your inner being with power through his Spirit, and that Christ may dwell in your hearts through faith, as you are being rooted and grounded in love. I pray that you may have the power to comprehend, with all the saints, what is the breadth and length and height and depth, and to know the love of Christ that surpasses knowledge, so that you may be filled with all the fullness of God. (Ephesians 3:16-19, NRSV)

Part One

Three Ways to Pray

1

Praying With Other People's Words

When Jesus gave his disciples this prayer, he was giving them part of his own breath, his own life, his own prayer.[2]

N.T. Wright

At one point in my life a few years ago, I noticed something that really troubled me: I was becoming less like my dad. I'd always had a lot of his character in me, but for a variety of reasons, I began noticing myself becoming more hurried and less patient. I was enjoying my work less, and often feeling like I had to pretend to be someone other than who I really was. All of these qualities were the opposite of the character of my dad. I noticed these things, but wasn't sure of what to do about them. The thought that I didn't like becoming more unlike my dad stayed with me for quite a while.

It was ironic that during that time of my life, my circumstances were very good: I had a loving, talented and beautiful wife (and still do), a baby boy whom I had quickly come to love more than I had ever thought possible (and still do, though he's no longer a baby), a good job in a good church, and much to my entire family's surprise, was enjoying living close to my parents after having lived other places for eleven years. The reason this surprised me so much was that, although I enjoyed growing up where I did in West Texas, it was never in my plans to go back. None of us ever know what's in store for us farther down the road, and things played out so that I, now with a delightful family, was again living close to my parents.

Part of the reason this was such a welcome surprise was that ever since I was a young boy, my dad, who was always my hero, had struggled with some serious health problems. He beat cancer when I was five, but then later fought through lupus and several other diseases, and eventually got cancer again. So, having always had the question of not knowing how much time we had left with him in the back of my mind, I was thrilled to be living close to him again at the time when my first child was born.

After my son's birth, my family had a wonderful year and a half of living close to my parents and seeing how much they and the new baby boy enjoyed one another. There's nothing quite like a new grandbaby living nearby to re-inject life into a house that had been home to empty nesters for more than a decade. It was during that time that I noticed my growing unlikeness to my dad and was troubled by it.

About halfway through the second year of living close to my parents, my dad was diagnosed with advanced esophageal cancer, of which he died six months later. Among the difficulties of the situation were my continuing realization that though I had always wanted to be more like him, I was heading in the opposite direction. Additionally, the fear that without him around, my unlikeness to him would only continue to grow. But again, we never know what's in store down the road, and the cure for my growing unlikeness to my dad came from an unexpected circumstance.

His illness forced me to begin to help more with the family farm and ranch business that he had been running for forty years. Even though it had been the family business for generations, I had never foreseen the possibility that I might someday become involved. Although I had grown up around the ranch and spent a lot of time with my dad there, I didn't know the first thing about running it.

Now, fast forward to about a year into being involved with my dad's business, when I noticed something that really pleased me: I was becoming more like him. I began noticing in myself more and more of the qualities I loved about my Dad: I was becoming less hurried, more patient, enjoying my work more, and often feeling like I was doing things that were deeply built in to who I was, all of which were qualities I loved about my Dad.

What reversed my path of becoming less like him and again helped his kind of character to continue growing in me? *I had been doing more of the things that he did, in order to become more of the kind of person he was.* As I repeatedly sat at his desk, used his tools, drove where he drove, dealt with people he dealt with, fed the cattle that he fed, and walked where he walked, it didn't really come as much of a surprise that I found myself living with more of the qualities he had.

Each of the ways of praying that we will explore in this book is important for this same reason. Throughout the centuries, millions of people who have known God have practiced these three ways of praying, including Jesus himself. It is in doing these things that they did that we can become the kind of people they were.

This is true of each of these three ways of praying, but I think it's most important with our first way to pray, praying with other people's words. This kind of prayer is very familiar to many of us and unfamiliar, even scary, territory to many others. Regardless of what your background with it may be, I hope that by the end of this chapter you will find deeper meaning in praying with other people's words. It overwhelms me to think that many, if not all, of our heroes of faith have prayed in this way. This is a primary way that we can do something they did in order to become the kind of people they were.

How Pipe Organs and Electric Guitars Shape Our Prayers

One aspect of my church that is somewhat uncommon is that we have two distinct worship services happening simultaneously in the same building each Sunday. If you were to walk through our building about five minutes after the beginning of the worship services, on one end of the hallway you would hear a huge pipe organ booming as that part of our congregation sings a hymn that is likely to be three to five hundred years old or older. Other parts of their worship service will likely include things like the people up front being in robes, praying by saying aloud one of the responsive readings from one of the Psalms in the back of the hymnal, or banners hanging in the sanctuary that are certain colors at certain times of the year.

If you would normally prefer to worship at this end of the hallway, my hope is that this chapter will add depth of meaning to some things you likely do in worship already, and help you to see ways that we could become more prayerful people by carrying those practices into the other parts of our days and weeks.

However, the worship service taking place at the other end of the hallway is very different. If you were to walk toward it, you would hear music equally booming, but this time coming from a drum set, guitars, and electric keyboards as that part of our congregation sings a song that is likely to be six months to a year old or newer. Other parts of their worship service will likely include things like the people up front being in jeans, every prayer being said spontaneously, and various multimedia images being projected on the majority of the wall space visible throughout the service.

If you would be more likely to find yourself in the drums and multimedia end of the hallway, this chapter might be a stretch for you. Thank you for at least reading to the fifth page of this chapter before skipping ahead in the book. Hang in there with me, because my experience is that you are likely to find at least as much depth of meaning in this way of praying as your friends down the hallway.

I mention this because I am well aware of the potential that some of you may already be turned off to this chapter just because of its title. If that is you, it's okay that you feel that way, and there is likely some good reason that you do. I am more of a newcomer to intentionally using this kind of prayer than the others that we will explore in this book, so I think I understand your hesitations. Yet I include this way of praying, and I include it first, for some important reasons. First, I have found this way of praying to be very life-giving to me personally, and as I have taught this material to others in classes and retreats, this way of praying is the one where people most often describe a light bulb coming on inside of them. One woman stopped me after we opened a retreat by teaching on the topics in this chapter and said, "Even if we didn't do anything else after that, I'm glad I came."

So, if you are one for whom the title "Praying With Other People's Words" fails to light a light bulb or anything else within you, remember the advice of Albert Haase's spiritual director that we considered in the Introduction: "Find the way of praying that works for you," the way of praying that helps you to be prayerful, and do so by trial and error. If praying with others' words isn't something that you think makes you tick, I am only asking you to hang in there with me through the end of the book and experiment with how each of these ways might help you become a more prayerful person.

What We've Lost by Losing Our Labels

During my lifetime, Christianity in our culture has seen quite a decline of what we might call denominationalism. I think much of the heart of that decline is a good thing. It's much less likely to meet someone of one Christian denomination who might not associate with you or consider you to have genuine faith in God simply for being of a particular denomination. We've come to be much more ready to recognize the fact that the tags we've given ourselves, such as Baptist, or

Methodist, or Presbyterian, or Catholic, do not in themselves say much about the quality of our love for God or lack thereof. The downside, however, is that the tags have also come to lose a great deal of meaning in how we shape our lives. The fact that everyone in the building where I attend church each week call ourselves Methodists says almost nothing today about the ways that we have learned to pray. Although there may be some positive aspects to the decline of denominationalism, this aspect is certainly to our loss, because we have a great deal to learn in the heritage that has been passed down to us.

A case study in my own tradition: I grew up in the more conservative, evangelical side of United Methodism. I'm extremely grateful for the evangelical churches in which I was raised, and the way that they emphasized my personal connection with God.

I remember praying the Lord's Prayer often in church growing up, but beyond that, I had the impression that if prayer was to be authentic and heartfelt, it had to be in my own words. I thought that to use prayers written by others was not only boring, but somehow lesser than addressing God spontaneously. In talking with others, this experience certainly isn't unique to me. Some of us have even been explicitly taught in our churches that the only time it might be acceptable to use other people's words in prayer is when we are brand new Christians and haven't yet learned how to pray "for ourselves." Or, perhaps it's also an acceptable substitute on those really dry days when we want to pray but just can't think of anything to say.

Author Scot McKnight talks about this in connection with his own discovery of praying with other people's words. He says,

> *We believed... that there was a spiritually dangerous connection between set prayers and impersonal faith... We were given this diagnosis for an argument: Repetition leads to recitation, and recitation leads to vain repetitions... Before long, we thought, we'd just be mouthing words and not meaning them at all. It is better, we were taught, to say something clumsy but really mean it from the heart than say something profound and poetic and run the risk of not meaning it. If meaninglessness meant vain repetition and meaningfulness meant spontaneous prayers, I would choose the second every time.*
>
> *But these are not the only two options.*
>
> *The Bible, Jesus, and the Church teach that we can learn to use set prayers at set times and... mean every word we say and, as a result, grow both personally and as a community of faith.*[3]

A great strength of John Wesley as he founded Methodism was to be able to hold two things together that seemed to be opposites, and to benefit from both. This is true in his own use of both spontaneous and written prayers. He was, not surprisingly, very methodical in his use of historic prayers, but also left space to say his own things to God, and so he felt that he had the best of both worlds. Wesley believed, practiced and taught the early Methodists that using historic, written prayers would enrich their understanding and expression of true prayer. He thought that doing so helped us to learn how to pray. We notice areas in these old prayers that don't receive enough attention in our own words to God. Our own words can often be individualized and self-centered, whereas praying with these words that so many others have used for so long connects us with other Christians today and throughout history in a very real way.[4]

That's one of my favorite things that has sunk in as I've begun learning to pray words that have been passed down to us: that not only am I praying these things that carry such depth of meaning, but I'm doing so together with scores of others around the world who pray the same words today and throughout the centuries.

So, enough with trying to get into it, what are words of other people that we want to use to pray, and how can we do so?

Praying the Lord's Prayer

Certainly, as followers of Christ, no other prayer is as central to us as the one that Jesus taught us. I know of no sense in which we can call ourselves followers of Jesus without taking very seriously the words he gave us when he said, "When you pray, pray like this, 'Our Father...'"

There is such depth in this prayer, that even if you've prayed it in church for years without meaning anything in your prayer, you still have a head start on learning this kind of prayer because its words have likely become deeply ingrained in you.

It speaks of our relationship with our heavenly Father, reminding us immediately that we pray this prayer together with all of Christ's followers, regardless of whether we're with a crowd in a sanctuary or alone in our room.

It reminds us that our Father is both here with us and everywhere in all of creation.

It states our desire that his name would be treasured and honored as it deserves.

It submits our wills, our little kingdoms, to the Father's great eternal kingdom.

It expresses our trust and dependence on the Father to give us the things that we need today to live our lives fully in him.

It reminds us that we are desperately in need of God's mercy, and that having received it, we cannot help but offer mercy to others.

It declares that we are not strong enough to face temptation and the time of trial on our own, but that we are in complete need of the Father's help to cleanse us and our world of evil.

It ascribes glory and power to the Father whose kingdom and whose name is on the line when we place our trust in him in such a radical way as Jesus instructs in this prayer.

That's a good prayer! We need it to sink as deeply into us as possible, and certainly one way of allowing that to happen is to pray it often.

I think it's interesting that we know even as early as 60 A.D., within a generation of Jesus' own life, even before much of the New Testament had been written, Christians were being instructed to pray these words of Jesus three times a day. Certainly we can benefit from doing the same, and we'll come back to a way to go about doing so in a few pages.

One way that I have found particularly helpful to be guided by Jesus' prayer is to allow it to focus my prayers for others and for myself. For example, let's say I am praying for my children. I can pray for them by saying,

Our Father in heaven, and be mindful and thankful that whether I'm with them or away from them, that God is present with and caring for them just as he is present with and caring for me.

I pray, *hallowed be thy name,* and I'm praying that God's name would be treasured and honored in their lives and in mine.

And I continue on through the prayer, being mindful of praying it for the other person. Then I can pray, *Thy kingdom come, thy will be done on earth, in Ethan and in Mia and in our family, just as it is in heaven,* praying that their lives in this world, today and always would be an extension of God's life among us.

And I pray, *Give us this day our daily bread,* praying that my little boy and my little girl would have all of the things they need today to live their lives fully in God: physically, emotionally, spiritually, relationally, in every way.

Forgive us our trespasses as we forgive those who trespass against us... At the time I am writing this, my son, Ethan, is three, and regardless of what time of day it is he may well have accumulated a need of forgiveness for some things. Mia, however is only four months old right now, so I don't think she has much to confess. Yet regardless of their age, I can still pray this for them, praying particularly that they would always know our home to be a place of forgiveness and mercy. They're going to mess up, and by praying this I'm in part praying that when that time comes, I'll be a forgiving father to them just as my Father has forgiven me.

Lead us not into temptation, but deliver us from evil. What better thing to pray for your children, or for whomever, than that they would be led along, not in the ways of the world around them, but in God's ways, and that they would be completely and fully delivered from all the kinds of evil that will ever be a threat to them every day of their lives?

For thine is the kingdom, the power, and the glory forever. These kids are my children, yet they are God's children. Just as my name is on the line in their lives, because we've entrusted them to God, his name is on the line with them too, and so I pray that their lives will, today and always, give him glory.

Often when praying this way, I have to stop and realize, "I just let those words run through my mind because they're memorized, rather than praying them." So I back up and pray them again. That's just part of the habit we need to develop whenever we pray with others' words. It will require some effort on our part to pay attention to the words that are before us and to really pray them. Yet when we do, we find that the shape it gives to our prayer and to our lives is invaluable.

Scot McKnight says, "Humans have a knack for turning religious acts into meaninglessness... If our prayers have become vain repetitions, it is because our heart is not engaged, not because of what we say."[5] And so, it will almost inevitably take some pausing and backing up in order to make sure that our heart is engaged.

Let's connect Jesus' prayer to an even older way of praying with other people's words.

Praying the Psalms

It is for good reason that the Psalms are often referred to as "the prayer book of the Bible," and often today we far underestimate the role that they have played for 4,000 years in shaping the prayer lives of God's people through the centuries. It was common practice among ancient Jews to have all 150 psalms memorized, largely in order to be able to call them to mind for prayer as individuals and also to guide their prayers when they were gathered together.

Most important for us as Christians is to realize how much the Psalms shaped the life and prayers of Jesus, and through him, also of the earliest Christians. The words of the Psalms that Jesus had prayed alone and within the Jewish community from the time he was a boy, as all Jewish boys did, were so deeply ingrained in him that we read of him speaking them throughout the gospels. For example, when Jesus says, "from the lips of children and infants you have ordained praise,"[6] "the stone the builders rejected has become the cornerstone,"[7] "blessed is he who comes in the name of the Lord,"[8] or "my God, my God, why have you forsaken me,"[9] he is quoting passages from the Psalms that guided him in prayer throughout his life.

And so for centuries, Jews and Christians have trusted the Psalms as a wonderful, rich, reliable guide for prayer. We'll take a closer look at how they have done so in a moment, but before we move on, perhaps you might want to make note of a way to experiment with praying a psalm with which you're likely already familiar.

In *The Good and Beautiful God*, James Bryan Smith suggests the practice of praying Psalm 23 as often as you can during one week:

"Try to recite Psalm 23 before you fall asleep each night, and again when you awake. Before your feet hit the ground, try to have slowly meditated on each word. Recite it so often this week that it becomes second nature to you, as natural as breathing. You will notice yourself beginning to pray it at odd times."[10]

Perhaps you'll want to make this your practice this week, and pray these words that have been prayed by innumerable people throughout history, including our Lord himself! (You can find Psalm 23 in the Guides for Prayer in Part Two of this book, as part of the prayer for Saturday Morning.)

Fixed-Hour Prayer

There's a particular method in which Christians throughout history have most commonly prayed the Lord's Prayer and the Psalms, as well as other prayers given to us by our fellow followers of Christ. This practice has several names. If you are like me, you may have done it at some time and not even realized it, but it's referred to by terms such as fixed-hour prayer, praying the office, praying the hours, or other similar names.

The fact that I've only recently learned this practice, and that I can mention it here without everyone reading this book already being well acquainted with it, signifies that we have drifted a long, long way from this method of praying that has been central to so many of the people who have ever called themselves followers of Jesus. Along with Holy Communion, it is the oldest surviving practice of Christian spirituality. The structure of the practice is that at set times of the day we pause to pray, or to "say our prayers," and this traditionally includes a heavy reliance on the Psalms, saying the Lord's Prayer, a time for silence, and other prayers that have long been central to Christian understanding and practice.

The roots of this way of praying with other people's words are seen in the Old Testament. For example, when Daniel is arrested and thrown into the lions' den, it is because he broke a law by going to his room "three times a day" to pray.

Or in the Psalms, we read references to praying in the evening, in the morning, and during the day. Psalm 118 says, "Seven times a day will I praise you," and people throughout the centuries have actually meant it! In monastic communities there are seven times of the day when the bells will ring to call the community to prayer, and they will gather and pray these ancient words.

For those outside of monasteries, it is more common to have between two and four times a day to have set hours for prayer, and the rhythm that this establishes in our lives is a constant reminder of God's presence, and of inestimable value in helping us to live prayerfully.

The practice was already in something like its present form in the day of Jesus, so again, this means that this way of prayer shaped the prayer life of our Lord himself and his early followers. Among the earliest Christians, Jew and Gentile alike also assumed it to be an important part of what it meant to follow him.

So, when we read things in the scriptures like in Acts 3, where "Peter and John were going up to the temple at the hour of prayer, at three o'clock in the afternoon," we are seeing how integral it was to Jesus and his disciples to practice fixed-hour prayer. Or, when the disciples were gathered together for prayer at nine in the morning when the Holy Spirit came at Pentecost, or when Peter went on his roof to pray at noon and had a vision from God, these are examples of how the lives of those who have gone before us have been arranged in order to learn to pray.

Fixed-hour prayer has continued to be a central part of Christian discipleship for centuries. Again, in my own tradition, Methodism would certainly not have been so methodical without the Wesleys' practice of morning and evening prayer. One writer said, "the daily office of Morning and Evening Prayer as set out in *The Book of Common Prayer* was the essence of John and Charles Wesley's 'method,' which also included scriptural study, fasting and regular reception of Holy Communion."[11]

It is only very recently in the history of Christianity, particularly in Protestantism in our culture, where this practice of praying, especially with the Psalms and the Lord's Prayer, has almost completely disappeared from the lives of so many Christians. Robert Benson has written a very good book on fixed-hour prayer, called *In Constant Prayer*, in which he reflects on this loss. He says,

> *Sometimes it occurs to me that I am a member of the first generation of followers of Yahweh in six thousand years for whom the offering of daily fixed-hour worship and praise and prayer—a tradition practiced and treasured and passed down to us from the Hebrews to the apostles to the early Christians to the fathers and mothers of the faith who sustained this Church we now call home—is no longer deemed a necessity or an obligation or even an opportunity. Sometimes when I*

think of that, I want to fall on my knees and maybe even on my face.[12]

And then he also says,

It occurs to me that if this way of prayer was good enough for the faithful to pray while waiting for the Messiah to come—alongside Moses and David and Jeremiah and the rest, if it was good enough for Jesus himself to have prayed when he was a young man, and if it was good enough for Paul and Peter and James and John, good enough for Abba Antony and Abba Theodore and Abba Pachomius in the desert, good enough for Saint Benedict and Saint Francis and Saint Hildegard and Saint Teresa, good enough for John Wesley and Martin Luther and Thomas Cranmer, it may well be good enough for me.[13]

An interesting thing about how people have viewed this throughout history is that it is a very practical way for the entire church to literally fulfill Paul's command to "pray without ceasing." Tomorrow morning after I wake up, the first thing I will do is to pray morning prayer. But I will do so only after Christians in Johannesburg said their morning prayers while I was fast asleep, and in the next hour another group in the next time zone will pray, and on and on through the night other Christians will wake up in their time zones, say their morning prayers, and then it will finally be our turn here in the USA's Central time zone. Then it repeats at mid-day, evening, and night, so that constantly, all throughout the world,

Christ's people are praying, and in a very real sense, doing so together and without ceasing.

Will This be Boring?

Now, after having built it up, let me give you a warning about beginning to practice this way of praying: you may do it and then not think it to be particularly special. That is just fine. Part of the reason that this way of prayer has disappeared from our practice is that we have come to evaluate our prayers and our worship by what we get out of them, yet that is not in any way the point. It sometimes happens that we receive gifts, such as a special awareness of God's presence, or something else good, but usually this is going to feel rather routine. Again, that's just fine. The act of submitting our souls to this kind of rhythm of prayer, benefiting from the prayer of Jesus and the prayers that have shaped so many of his followers, will surely have an effect on us over time, but it mostly happens at a level deeper than our feelings.

St. John of the Cross wrote about this hundreds of years ago, but it sounds like he is describing our generation today:

> *The problem is this: when they have received no pleasure for their devotions, they think they have not accomplished anything. This is a grave error, and it judges God unfairly. For the truth is that the feelings we receive from our devotional life are the least of its benefits. The invisible and unfelt grace of God is much greater, and it is beyond our comprehension.*[14]

So, as we pray in this way, one of our challenges is to understand that routine is not just okay, but even very good, because of the great work that God is doing "beyond our comprehension" as we regularly submit ourselves to him through this method of prayer.

The Power of Shared Vocabulary

Business and organizational leaders have long recognized the value of developing a shared vocabulary among a group of people. Shared vocabulary helps unite us around our common values, goals and understandings. For us as Christians, these prayers that have been given to us by the people of God throughout history, and by Jesus himself, are our shared prayer vocabulary.

My grandfather often used to say, "That's the spirit" whenever one of us had a good attitude about something. I was only around this grandfather once or twice per year as a child, but this was *the* phrase I came to associate with him. He didn't just say it once or twice, but it seemed like any time that we did something he liked, his repetitive response was, "That's the spirit."

Now, without ever having made a conscious decision to do so, you can guess what I say to my children when they have a good attitude: "That's the spirit." The words aren't original to me, and someone else probably said them to my grandfather before he ever said them to us. Whenever I'm together with one of my brothers and one of us says, "That's the spirit," we are instantly on the same page with one another. Through repetition over time, it has become part of our shared vocabulary and a mark of our connection to one another as family.

This morning, when I prayed "O God, make speed to save us," and "Our Father, who art in heaven," I was praying with words that are not my own, but that have been passed on to me through countless generations. They are one of the most important marks that I belong to this family, and through repetition over time, they will continue to shape me to be more like Jesus and all of our Father's people who have prayed them all over the world through every day of our family's history.

Praying With Other People's Words

For Further Praying
- *A Pocket Guide to Prayer* by Steve Harper
- *The Divine Hours* by Phyllis Tickle
  (Online version: explorefaith.org / prayer / fixed /)

For Further Reading
- *In Constant Prayer* by Robert Benson
- *Praying With the Church* by Scot McKnight

Also see salvationlife.com for other recommended resources.

2

Praying
Without Words

We are starved for quiet,
to hear the sound of sheer silence that is the presence of God himself.[15]

Ruth Haley Barton

I really like to not talk. It is only by God's mercy that my wife married me. She later admitted that when she first met me in college, she was surveying a group of guys and came to the conclusion about me: "He's the cutest but he doesn't talk." So she passed me by for a couple of years.

Being a quiet person is relative, though. People who knew both my father and me realize that he made me look like an incessant blubberer. He certainly preferred to use very few words, and being quiet was ingrained in the way I was raised on a West Texas ranch. A family legend that was passed down to me consists of my Granddad and my Uncle Tig sitting on the porch after working on the ranch.

Granddad: "It sure is hot today."

Five minutes passed.

Uncle Tig: "Yep. Sure is."

I'll admit right off the bat that compared to most people, I'm more comfortable with and more drawn to things that don't involve talking, and I think it is true that our personality preferences are something to pay attention to in the spiritual life. For example, if I go on a retreat and I hear that it's going to involve time in solitude, I'm disappointed if it's less than five hours. On the other hand, I have two friends named Paul who both are every bit as extroverted as I am introverted. They would each be ready to leave the retreat center on foot and find someone, *anyone*, to talk to after about ten minutes of being alone. Neither preference is better than the other, but it's good to pay attention to our preferences when we talk about ways to pray, because we can give each other grace. If I meet you and do not make much conversation, paying attention to our preferences can mean that you will give me grace in understanding that my lack of words does not indicate that I dislike you; then I can give you extroverts grace, refraining from thinking you to be unspiritual when I see you twitch at the mention of solitude.

Even though our personality preferences may have some influence, I am convinced that praying without words is neither an "introvert thing" nor an "extrovert thing." The reality is that this way of praying is very stretching for all of us, and that's precisely why the church has hung on to it as a central Christian practice through the centuries, and why we need so desperately to rediscover its practice today. Ruth Haley Barton says, "silence is the most challenging, the most needed and the least experienced spiritual discipline among evangelical Christians today."[16]

I think she's right, and if it's the most challenging, the most needed, and the least experienced spiritual discipline for us today, it's going to be stretching for all of us. It will probably be more obvious that silence is stretching to extroverts, because we might see them fidgeting, texting someone on their phones, or climbing the retreat center walls during solitude time, but the reality of the practice is that praying without words is just as stretching for introverts like me as it is for my friends named Paul.

I am extremely comfortable not having to say anything with my mouth, not having people around me saying anything, and being wrapped up in my own thoughts. That's the place where I spend the huge majority of my life. Even though my mouth may be still, silent prayer stretches me because the challenge is to get this world of thoughts where I am so comfortable to slow down, be quiet and rest in the awareness of God's presence.

As I've read the thoughts of many people who have practiced prayer in various ways throughout history, many of them attest to the fact that in prayer, regardless of how practiced we become, there is a real sense in which none of us will ever be anything but beginners. I think that's particularly true in praying without words. It will challenge all of us in some very deep places. So, we have to remember that great advice mentioned in the previous chapter from St. John of the Cross and give up our obsession with how the practice *feels* to us. Part of what he said was how great the "invisible and unfelt grace of God is," and how the work that it does in places in us that are beyond our awareness is an essential part of the spiritual life.

Thomas Merton is one of the teachers most often associated with praying without words. He says that this kind of prayer "is sometimes quite difficult. If we bear with hardship in prayer and wait patiently for the time of grace, we may well discover that meditation and prayer are very joyful experiences. We should not, however, judge the value of our meditation by 'how we feel.' A hard and apparently fruitless meditation may in fact be much more valuable than one that is easy, happy, enlightened, and apparently a big success."[17]

So Why Bother with It?

If praying without words is going to be contrary to our feelings like that, and if it's going to stretch us so much, why bother with it?

Maybe we can understand the need for practicing prayer without words in our relationship with God if we think of times without words with our loved ones. Something about our relationships helps us to understand that it can be a sign of maturity to be able to enjoy being together while not saying anything.

My father was my hero, and I already mentioned how quiet he was. When I graduated from high school, I had the idea that it would be fun for the two of us to make the six-hour drive to the Dallas-Fort Worth Metroplex to see a Texas Rangers baseball game together. Their new ballpark had just opened, and he'd never been to a major league game, so we went. He and I drove there in his pickup truck the day of the game, watched it, stayed the night in a hotel, drove back the next day, and I don't think we said more than 150 words on the whole trip.

And for the rest of his life we still mentioned how much we enjoyed that trip!

You are likely not as quiet as my father and I, but I think you can understand something of this aspect of a relationship between people. There comes a point in getting to know someone when you can enjoy just being together rather than having to get acquainted through small talk and other conversation. Sure, words are still fine and are often used, but there is also a trust and comfort that is uniquely expressed without them.

Brennan Manning says, "Simply showing up is a kind of loving. The readiness to conscientiously waste time with a friend is a silent affirmation of their importance in our lives."[18] That is a great description of what prayer without words is: "conscientiously wasting time with a friend to affirm their importance in our lives."

I had been a Christian for quite a while before I ever realized the truth of this in my relationship with God. It occurred to me, "If I cannot enjoy just being with God, without having to fill the time with words or other things, what does that say about how close we are? How can I even really describe it as a relationship, much less an 'intimate personal relationship' like we often say, if I will so easily come up with any tool or excuse available to avoid just being with God?"

Dallas Willard describes this bluntly. He says, "Silence is frightening because it strips us as nothing else does, throwing us upon the stark realities of our life. It reminds us of death, which will cut us off from this world and leave only us and God. And in that quiet, what if there turns out to be very little to 'just us and God'? Think of what it says about the emptiness of our inner lives if we must always turn on the tape player or radio to make sure something is happening around us."[19]

Praying without any words is such an important part of the spiritual life because our time in prayer without words is the time when that "something between just me and God" is given a chance to grow and develop. It is the time when what we so often call a relationship with God can come to consist of the two of us actually enjoying being together.

Albert Haase recounts a great story of a 19th century parish priest in France. One of the first things the priest noticed after coming to town was a certain villager who never passed the church without entering. He would enter the church in the morning on the way to work and again on his return home in the evening, leaving his pickaxe at the door. The priest also noticed that the villager never prayed with rosary beads or a prayer book, so he once asked the man what he said to God during his long visits in the church. The man answered, "Oh, I don't say anything to God... I look at God and God looks at me."[20]

I want to know God in that kind of way. Unfortunately, though, we live in a very noisy world that makes it quite a challenge to do so.

Silence and Our Ability to Hear from God

In 1 Kings 19, the prophet Elijah was running for his life from Queen Jezebel. After lying down to die under a tree in the desert, an angel of God came to give him food and water to strengthen him for a journey which he had not intended to take. After food, drink and rest, Elijah journeyed to Mount Horeb and spent the night in a cave.

While there, God asked Elijah, "What are you doing here?"

Elijah's response was, "I have been very zealous for the Lord, the God of hosts; for the Israelites have forsaken your covenant, thrown down your altars, and killed your prophets with the sword. I alone am left, and they are seeking my life, to take it away."

Then the story continues in verses 11-13, "[God] said, 'Go out and stand on the mountain before the Lord, for the Lord is about to pass by.' Now there was a great wind, so strong that it was splitting mountains and breaking rocks in pieces before the Lord, but the Lord was not in the wind; and after the wind an earthquake, but the Lord was not in the earthquake; and after the earthquake a fire, but the Lord was not in the fire; and after the fire a sound of sheer silence. When Elijah heard it, he wrapped his face in his mantle and went out and stood at the entrance of the cave."

Elijah had come to know God well enough to recognize that God's presence was in "the sound of sheer silence."

In a *Nooma* video titled "Noise," Rob Bell applies this passage to us. He does a great job of pointing out that although God is often in the silence, for some reason silence is very hard for us to deal with. He talks about how accustomed we are to all kinds of noise in our lives, and how this easily crowds out our ability to hear from God. Every time I watch the video, I feel deeply challenged when the question is asked, "Does my life look like that of someone who really wants to hear God's voice?"[21]

I think there is something very important for us to understand in this connection between silence and hearing from God. Learning to listen for God is an important aspect of praying without words. Some people even primarily refer to this kind of praying as "listening prayer." I have come to be convinced that praying without words is a very helpful practice for learning to hear from God, but I also believe that praying without words and hearing God do not have the direct correlation that we often expect.

I can remember a time when I had my first staff position at a church, and I was facing a decision that felt fairly urgent at the time and I really wanted to have God's guidance in what I should do. So I went into the church sanctuary one afternoon by myself and sat up near the altar to pray. I had the idea that if I could just get my mind quiet enough, then I would be able to hear God speaking something to me. I wasn't expecting any audible voice, but I thought that if I could really enter into silence, God would then speak.

I absolutely think there's a connection between practicing silence and hearing God, but the problem when we come with the approach that I had, really expecting that God will speak to us at a certain time in a certain way, is that we will be likely to force a word from God which isn't really from God at all. That experience in the sanctuary wasn't unique in my younger days. I repeatedly left times of prayer convinced that I had received communication from God, but life circumstances would play out to let me know unmistakably that I had been wrong.

Just as the point of having specific times of prayer is to make us more prayerful, not just in the time of prayer, but more so throughout the rest of our day, the point of prayer without words (or listening prayer) is to make us more attentive to God, particularly in the rest of the day that we spend doing something other than being in a time set aside for prayer.

Another experience from several years ago illustrates this. I was in my first year out of college, had taken a job in Georgia, and was living by myself. I had just started reading about prayer without words and had begun trying to practice it for a couple of months. In reading about it, I came across some of the most helpful advice I've ever heard about prayer. Richard Foster said, "In the beginning it is wise to strive for uneventful prayer experiences."[22] In other words, his advice was to go into the sanctuary and pray and seek for my mind and heart to become quiet, but expect it to be uneventful and to feel like a waste of time, rather than expecting God to answer me right then and there. That freed me from the need to leave the sanctuary having forced something from God. In fact, it gave me motivation to learn to be quiet with God and to be okay hearing nothing from God, even *seeking* to hear nothing from him.

It seems like odd and counterintuitive advice, but here's why it's so dependable: After a couple of months of completely uneventful prayer experiences, I was at home alone one evening and had rented the Denzel Washington movie *The Hurricane*. If you haven't seen it and don't want a spoiler, skip the next few paragraphs. The movie is based on the true story of boxer Rubin "Hurricane" Carter being wrongly imprisoned for murder. A group of lawyers finds out about his story and tries to help him, but appeal after appeal is rejected. One of the scenes in the courtroom has things proceeding as they have been in all of their attempts to get the verdict reversed, then suddenly, just when it appears that another rejection is coming, the judge announces that Carter's conviction had been based on racism rather than reason, and the courtroom erupts when the judge says, "I hereby order Rubin Carter released from prison...."

At that moment, while I was watching the movie, as clear as any communication from God that I've ever known, the Lord communicated, "That's exactly what I've done for you." I had been imprisoned to my sin, my loneliness, and a way of life separated from God, and then because of what God has done for me, I knew that I was in a very real sense set free from my prison.

It wasn't until years later that I realized the connection between the way that I had been practicing prayer without words and the profound experience of God's communication with me while watching a movie. It is uneventful times dedicated to prayer that make us prayerful in the rest of the day, and it's uneventful, dedicated times of praying without words that make us more attentive to God's word in the rest of our lives.

Dealing With Distractions

As we try to work the practice of praying without words into our lives, one of the first obstacles we will run into is dealing with our own distractions. We will likely begin our prayer thirsty for time with God, and for the first few seconds we may be able to enjoy how great of a thing it is that we are able to enjoy just being with God. And then, about 15 seconds into this joyful experience, we realize how urgent it is that we have to make a certain phone call; or some task around the house has to get done *right now*; or, you know, that spot on the wall really looks like it's in the shape of Abraham Lincoln's face; or any of a million other things. The distractions can be random wanderings of our imagination like those, or they may be something more emotionally charged, like the way someone made us angry lately, or we may even have some great psychological or theological insight that comes to us. "Oh, I have to teach this thing that I just realized in Sunday School!"

Henri Nouwen says that when we try to pray without words, the way our minds work is like they're a tree full of monkeys jumping in a banana tree.[23] All of these distractions come rushing at us, making all of their noise and jumping up and down. Then, the best spiritual advice of the ages says that we should know that the monkeys are there, and just wait and let the monkeys settle down.

There will certainly be days that we're more effective at this than others, but along the same line of advice as striving for uneventful prayer experiences, Thomas Keating urges us that if we notice a time of prayer being good, or being bad, that we need to give up those kinds of categories altogether.[24] Praying without words is not an area of our lives where we need to subject ourselves to constant evaluation, because I am absolutely sure that the distractions are a much bigger bother to us than they are to God.

When my son, Ethan, was about eighteen months old, I was playing with him one afternoon in our backyard. I was sitting on our porch swing, and Ethan was playing with toys in the grass. I love it when he wears his cowboy hat, and he really liked wearing it that day. I was enjoying watching him play, and then at times, he would put his toy down, come climb up in the swing next to me and just sit next to his daddy on the swing, wearing his cowboy hat. Then, pretty quickly, he would see something else he wanted to play with, get down, and play with it for a while. Then, again, he would crawl back in the swing with me, and the cycle kept repeating.

My heart felt so full that afternoon. I loved it that even though he had his toys there and enjoyed playing with them, he still wanted at times to come sit with his daddy on the swing, wearing his cowboy hat. The fact that something else would quickly grab his attention didn't bother me in the least. He was only a year and a half old, and I was much more capable of enjoying his company than he was mine, but it still made my heart want to burst with joy and pride over that little guy when he did turn his attention to me and wanted to be by my side.

I'm so thankful for the imagery in the scriptures that teaches us that we are God's children. When we pray without words, the distractions are going to come, but we just let them float by as if they were clouds in the sky that we notice momentarily, but don't allow our attention to hang on to them. Then, we crawl back up in the swing and return our attention to our Father.

Basil Pennington describes something very like my experience with Ethan:

> A father is delighted when his little one, leaving off his toys and friends, runs to him and climbs into his arms. As he holds the little one close to him, he cares little about whether the child is looking around, his attention flitting from one thing to another, or just settling down to sleep. Essentially the child is choosing to be with his father, confident of the love, the care, the security, that is there in those arms. Contemplative prayer

is much like that. We settle down into our
Father's arms, in his loving hands. Our mind, our
thoughts, our imagination may flit about here and
there; we might even fall asleep; but essentially we
are choosing to remain for this time intimately
with our Father, giving ourselves to him,
receiving his love and care, letting him enjoy us as
he will. It is very simple prayer. It is very childlike
prayer. It is prayer that opens us up to all the
delights of the Kingdom.[25]

As I mentioned earlier, it has been very beneficial for
me to learn to combine these three ways to pray, so the
guides for prayer in Part Two of this book combine
praying with other people's words, praying without
words, and praying with your own words. Instructions
are included there, but be aware that there is an
indicated pause for silence after the scripture reading to
practice praying without words. Use this time to enjoy
being quiet, together with God, "conscientiously wasting
time" with your Father. Remember, distractions will
come, and they bother you more than they bother God.
When you realize you've drifted, just bring your
attention back to God's presence as if you were a little
boy in a cowboy hat crawling back up into the swing to
sit next to his daddy. You will make his heart feel full.

Praying Without Words

For Further Praying

- Visit <u>www.contemplativeoutreach.org</u> for resources and events designed to help people learn to pray without words.

For Further Reading

- *Invitation to Solitude and Silence* by Ruth Haley Barton

Also see salvationlife.com for other recommended resources.

3

Praying With
Your Own Words

"Draw near to God and he will draw near to you." That is astonishing! God is ready and waiting. He longs to establish a friendship with you, a friendship deeper, stronger, and more satisfying than you can ever imagine. This, too, will take time, as any friendship worthy of the name will do. But what could be more worthwhile? If even a few more people were prepared to take these promises seriously, think what a difference it would make to the world.[26]

N.T. Wright

I recently bought a bigger pickup truck, solely for the purpose of being able to take my kids around with me when I'm doing work on our ranch. I love it when I get to take them. Sure, my productivity takes a dramatic nosedive, but I can still get some things done, and I love having my favorite people (my family) with me at my favorite place (our ranch).

I had my three-year-old son with me on one of these days, and on our way out of town driving toward the ranch we had to stop at a tire shop and get a flat tire fixed. After it was finished, and as I was buckling my little boy back into his car seat, we had a short conversation that I hope I never forget:

Me: I sure love having you with me, Bud.

Him: I love having you with me, too, Daddy. I wouldn't want to go anywhere without ya.

…[He thought for a minute as I continued buckling him in]…

Him: If you were going somewhere by yourself, I'd want to catch up.

Now *that* will make any daddy's day. In fact, that conversation took place almost a year ago, so I guess I can say that it didn't just make my day, but made my year.

Out of the three ways of praying that we explore in this book, I grew up most accustomed to this third way, praying with my own words. Although it was the most familiar to me when I was younger (and there's a good chance that's also the case for many of you reading this), in recent years I've focused more on the other two ways of praying.

Praying with other people's words through practices like Fixed-Hour Prayer has brought a shape, rhythm and depth to my prayer practices for which I had longed for for years.

Praying without words seems to be one of the most needed practices in my own spiritual life, and probably is for many of us. It's in doing so that what we so often call "a personal relationship with God," for me, becomes something that can actually be described as a relationship.

But these comments from my little boy, and the immense joy that they brought to me, knowing that they came from a very sincere place in his tender little heart, have reminded me of the power of talking to God in very personal words. For a lot of people, this is a very natural and easy way to pray, but it's not always for me, at least not at this point in my life.

I don't know if my words to God can have anywhere close to the same effect on him that my son's can have on me, but I would guess that it's similar. It certainly isn't by accident that the writers of scripture, and particularly Jesus, so often choose to describe our relationship to God as one between a loving father and his children. So, if things between God and me are similar to things between my son and me, I need to tell him how much I like being with him.

It doesn't require many words, but I've got to use some.

The Prayer All-Stars, Why I'm Not One of Them, and Why That's Okay

I haven't said much in the first two chapters generally about why we pray, or even what prayer is or the difference it makes in us and in the world. We'll do a little of that in this chapter, as we prepare to explore and experience prayer in our own words.

One of my favorite stories about a prayerful person is a story about George Müller. Some of you may recognize his name. He became fairly well known for his work with orphans in England in the 1800s. He decided from the outset of his ministry that he would never ask for financial support for his orphanage. He would simply ask God to provide for his needs and trust that God would do so.

By the end of his life, Müller's orphanages had cared for more than 10,000 children, and he had established 117 schools which provided education to more than 120,000 students. He was so effective at educating poor children that he was actually accused of "raising the poor above their natural station in life." And all of this was through an extremely prayerful man who was radically dependent on God.

The story goes that Müller was on a ship sailing for America when they came into a dense fog.

Because of it the captain had remained on the bridge continuously for twenty-four hours, when Mr. Müller came to him and said, "Captain, I have come to tell you that I must be in Quebec on Saturday afternoon." When informed that it was impossible, he replied: "Very well. If the ship cannot take me, God will find some other way. I have never broken an engagement for fifty-seven years. Let us go down into the chartroom and pray."

The captain continues the story thus: "I looked at that man of God and thought to myself, What lunatic asylum could that man have come from. I never heard such a thing as this." "Mr. Müller," I said, "do you know how dense the fog is?" "No," he replied, "my eye is not on the fog, but on the living God, who controls every circumstance of my life." He knelt down and prayed one of those simple prayers, and when he had finished I was going to pray; but he put his hand on my shoulder and told me not to pray. "Firstly," he said, "because you do not believe God will, and secondly, I believe God has, and there is no need whatever for you to pray about it." I looked at him, and George Müller said, "Captain, I have known my Lord for fifty-seven years, and there has never been a single day that I have failed to get an audience with the King. Get up and open the door, and you will find that the fog has gone." I got up and the fog was indeed gone. George Müller was in Quebec Saturday afternoon for his engagement.[27]

Isn't that great? I love to read stories of some of the "prayer giants" like that. For more than 50 years, John Wesley awoke between 4:00 and 5:00 a.m. for prayer. He said that he often had so much to do in a day that he could not afford not to spend at least three hours in prayer.

I have read stories about men and women like that for years, and for a long time I imagined that if I was ever going to be teaching others about prayer, my doing so would be full of stories like theirs, trying to inspire us to imitate their efforts.

The main obstacle that keeps me from trying to inspire others to imitate the efforts of the Müllers and Wesleys of history is simple: *I* can't imitate their efforts. I tried to pray like Wesley *once*. I gave up on day two, because, man, I was tired. To be someone who prays for hours every day, and sees things happen like fog disappearing from Müller's ship ... I have started to believe that those kinds of experiences may never happen to me, nor most of us. It's interesting that while Wesley and others like him certainly urged others to pray, they generally never encouraged others to pray in the ways that they did.

At this point in my life, I think I'm okay never making it into the prayer hall of fame. I don't need to become a superhero and have extraordinary experiences (although of course I would welcome them if they did happen). Instead, what I really, deeply desire is simply to keep becoming a more prayerful person. Remember again the story of Albert Haase from our Introduction, whose spiritual director told him, "our prayers are supposed to make us prayerful," meaning that the point of the times that we set aside for prayer is to be more able and likely to pray and be aware of God's presence through the rest of our day. We pray during some parts of each day so that the rest of every day can be lived prayerfully.

Therefore, please understand that we don't do the kinds of things we discuss in this book in order to try to become the prayer all-stars. Rather, my hope is simply that we can learn time-proven ways of praying that have been helpful to other followers of Jesus for a very long time, some of whom we may know by name, but the huge majority of whom were never known beyond the people around them.

I still think it's good to be inspired by stories of people like Müller and Wesley, but I hope that none of us have prayer's equivalent of football's all-pro quarterback in mind when we think of what it would mean to live a prayerful life. If we're going to associate a word with the lives of God's prayerful ones, I think it is much more helpful to us, and much more consistent with the message of the scriptures, to get rid of images and words like superstar or hero, and replace them with another, much simpler word: *friend*.

The scriptures give us various ways of understanding how God looks at us: they teach us that we are God's children, God's servants, Jesus' disciples, the bride of Christ, the body of Christ, or simply God's people. But there's another image that Jesus gave us on his last night with his disciples: he said in John 15: "I no longer call you servants, for a servant does not know his master's business. Instead, I have called you friends, for everything that I have learned from my Father I have made known to you."

I can sum up my motivation and desire to live prayerfully pretty well with a statement like this: I want to learn to pray, and live prayerfully, because I want to live my life as God's friend.

Perhaps friendship with God isn't a perfect way of understanding our relation to God, just as none of the metaphors we mentioned before are perfect and complete. I suppose that's why we have so many of them. Yet being God's friend communicates something very meaningful about what kind of lives we can expect to lead as we become more prayerful.

Think for a moment about the best relationship with a friend you have had. What are some of the qualities that made it exceptional? Among other qualities, there was almost certainly a level of trust. You understood one another. You simply enjoyed being together.

Also, I expect that my good friends want to hear from me and communicate with me. They want to know what things are important in my life right now, and I want to hear their feedback.

There are many definitions of prayer out there, but the one I like the best for the way of praying that we're looking at in this chapter is from Dallas Willard. He says, prayer is "talking to God about what we are doing together."[28]

Praying with our own words is an essential part of developing our friendship with God, and, as Willard points out, friends do things together. If we do nothing together with God, we will likely have little to say to one another, and we certainly could not characterize our relationship as a friendship.

Simple Prayer

One way to pray with our own words like this is what Richard Foster calls "Simple Prayer." Simple Prayer is, simply, talking with God about whatever is on our minds.

Foster describes Simple Prayer this way:

...we bring ourselves before God just as we are, warts and all. Like children before a loving father, we open our hearts and make our requests. We do not try to sort things out, the good from the bad. We simply and unpretentiously share our concerns and make our petitions. We tell God, for example, how frustrated we are with the co-worker at the office or the neighbor down the street. We ask for food, favorable weather, and good health.

In a very real sense we are the focus of Simple Prayer. Our needs, our wants, our concerns dominate our prayer experience. Our prayers are

*shot through with plenty of pride, conceit, vanity,
pretentiousness, haughtiness, and general all-
around egocentricity. No doubt there are also
magnanimity, generosity, unselfishness, and
universal goodwill.*[29]

He points out that this simple kind of prayer, just
praying what is on our minds, is the most common form
of prayer in the Bible. Think of all the complaints of
Moses, that good friend of God, or David and the other
writers of the Psalms. It is all throughout the stories of
scripture, and all throughout the lives of God's friends in
every part of history. It isn't sophisticated, it isn't pretty,
it isn't poetic. It's just "ordinary people bringing
ordinary concerns to a loving and compassionate
Father."[30]

For people as self-centered as we are, it isn't wise to
avoid a prayer before God because we think it will
sound self-centered. Foster says that "the only way we
move beyond 'self-centered prayer' (if indeed we ever
do) is by going through it, not by making a detour
around it."[31]

In Simple Prayer, we pray with our own words to
God about the ordinary events of our lives, or whatever
it is that has our attention. Foster offers these
suggestions: "For now, do not worry about 'proper'
praying, just talk to God. Share your hurts, share your
sorrows, share your joys—freely and openly. God listens
in compassion and love, just like we do when our
children come to us. He delights in our presence. When
we do this, we will discover something of inestimable
value. We will discover that by praying we learn to
pray."[32]

Sometimes we desire something more sophisticated in prayer, but to leave all the stuff of life out of our prayer is to not develop a friendship. So to write much more about this way of praying would be to deny the simplicity of it. Prayer with our own words, Simple Prayer, is "talking with God about what we are doing together." There's not a whole lot more to say about this type of prayer, so here is a brief suggestion: in this way of prayer just as much as in any other, we will have to deal with those monkeys in the banana tree, because our mind will wander just as much when we pray with our own words as it does during our other kinds of prayer. A simple way of dealing with the distractions while praying with our own words is to say your prayer aloud, or to write it. Obviously some privacy is helpful—particularly if you want to go with the vocal option.

Prayers That Spring From the Scriptures

Though Simple Prayer can encompass all that we need to say in praying with our own words, I also want to touch on another option for this way of prayer. I find that I often need something to give me a starting point, or a springboard, in using my own words in prayer. In *Laugh Your Way to a Better Marriage*, Mark Gungor talks about how men have something he calls a "nothing box."[33] That's the place that we like to go whenever possible, and the honest reply when you ask us what we're thinking about is, "nothing." Just like my wife usually has to use some questions to get me talking, even in prayer I often need something to get my words started. Otherwise, it's as if I'm asked:

"Do you want to talk to God?"

"Sure."

"What do you want to talk to God about?"

"Well, I don't know."

Whether you're male or female, and whether you often find yourself in a nothing box or not, this kind of praying with your own words will also be helpful for those of us for whom Simple Prayer may not have enough structure.

The following is adapted from Dallas Willard's book, *Hearing God*. He did not particularly write this in the context of a discussion on prayer, but rather on reading the scriptures. However, following these guidelines has been one of the most helpful ways for me to focus my times of prayer with my own words. Since he's talking about how to approach reading the scriptures, this kind of praying starts with a passage of scripture and leads us into praying with our own words.

- First, come to your chosen passage as to a place where you will have a holy meeting with God. Then, the remaining guidelines can be good starting points for continuing in prayer through each section using your own words.

- Look for *information*: if we are reading Psalm 23, "The Lord is my shepherd...," we might express the information in our prayer as, "David knew you, Lord, as his shepherd...."

- Express your *longing* for it to be so: "I wish the Lord were my shepherd. I want to know you that way, God..."

- *Affirmation* that it must be so: "It must be like that for me. Lord, I need to know you as my shepherd..."

- *Invocation* to God to make it so: "Lord, be my shepherd. Care for me and protect me. Guide me in the right ways..."

- *Appropriation* by God's grace that it is so: This is a settled conviction from deep within that it is a statement of fact about you. "Lord, you are my shepherd. I lack nothing under your care..." Willard wisely notes, "Do not rush this part! Let it take as long as it needs to take."[34]

As I mentioned, for this process to be meaningful for me, I almost always have to write my words. I have a journal that I use for this, and something similar may be helpful for you. Going through this process with a passage of scripture has helped me to express my own words to God in ways that I would not have been able to otherwise. It helps me to be able to "talk with God about what we are doing together," and just as importantly, it allows the scripture passage to sink much more deeply into me than it would if I had only read the words on the page.[35]

When Our Friendship Grows

The day when my son told me, "If you were going somewhere by yourself, I'd want to catch up" was a day worth remembering for me. He is older now than when he said those words to me, and though he's still very young, there are already times when he is beginning to want some distance from me rather than being right by my side. And adolescence hasn't even hit yet. Although I hope it never happens, there may well come a period of time when he doesn't want much to do with me. But his own words to me that day when he was three years old came from a very sincere place in his little soul, a place that knew he was loved, that his daddy delighted in him, and that it was a good thing for the two of us to ride around in our pickup truck together. Whatever the future may hold for us as father and son, I will always know that place in his soul is real and is still there, even if one of these days he completely stops paying attention to it.

There have been times in my years of seeking to follow God when, whether in joy or pain, I have expressed my love for God in sincere and authentic ways through using my own words in prayer. I've come to believe that those words delighted God in much the same way that my son's delighted me. There have also been times in my years of seeking to follow God when, like a confused or rebellious son, I didn't want to have much to do with him. Thankfully, though, even when those times came, I was eventually able to go back to words that came from a very sincere place in my soul that knows I am loved, that God delights in me, and that it is very good for us to do things together. Looking back over the decades, I can see that it's when I talk to God about everyday things in my own words that our friendship grows.

Praying With Your Own Words

For Further Praying
• *Contemplative Bible Reading* by Richard Peace

For Further Reading
• *Hearing God* by Dallas Willard

Also see salvationlife.com for other recommended resources.

The Making of
Prayerful People

*The secret to a life of prayer, by and large,
is showing up.*[36]

Robert Benson

My first sincere attempts as a youth at growing toward a prayerful life were by praying with my own words. Other than when we said the Lord's Prayer in worship services, this was the only way of prayer that I knew, so it was the only way that I prayed for many years.

In my first years after college, I enjoyed the discovery of reading spiritual writers who taught about praying without words. For a time, that became my primary way of praying, though by then praying with my own words was deeply ingrained enough in me that I could not completely let go of it.

About a decade later, while I sat at a Transforming Community retreat and listened to Ruth Haley Barton teach on fixed-hour prayer, I felt my soul being drawn like a magnet to the kind of prayer she described. I had experienced it in the Transforming Community and other places without even knowing what it was we were doing. As Ruth taught us this centuries-old way of praying with other people's words, I was eager to explore it and shape my life around it.

Upon returning home from the retreat, I immediately bought a copy of *The Divine Hours* by Phyllis Tickle and began a rhythm of praying with other people's words through fixed-hour prayer. I immediately noticed how it became a valuable bridge for me. Being a new parent, I often had days when the craziness of adapting to life with a baby in the house meant that my normal space for praying without words and praying with my own words was pushed aside. Yet with the constant rhythm of fixed-hour prayer, I was able to bridge those gaps.

As I became more familiar with the rhythm of praying with other people's words through fixed-hour prayer, I began to experiment with incorporating times of praying without words and praying with my own words into those established times of prayer. I experienced synergy.

Having benefited from each of these three ways of praying, initially each independently of the others, I was surprised to notice the difference it made when I put them together. I felt like every part of me was becoming more open to God, like I was finally getting a taste of the kind of prayerful life I had always wanted.

I can't say for sure whether or not your experience will be the same. In some ways, it certainly will not. But I can say that since I have found God's grace to be available so abundantly through these three ways of praying passed down to us from countless numbers of followers of Jesus throughout history, I am reasonably certain that you will find God's grace awaiting you too.

I said in the Introduction that a prayerful life is meant for everyone. Here in the Conclusion, I want to add to that statement and say: a prayerful life is meant for everyone, and none of us becomes prayerful by ourselves. Perhaps the synergy that surpasses that of putting together practices of praying with other people's words, praying without words, and praying with your own words is that of putting these practices together with others. It might be on a retreat, in a small group, or with your family, but the only way we are meant to live prayerfully is to live prayerfully together. Part Two of this book is a guide that you and others can use to do so.

I am deeply grateful to any of you who have read this far, and from this point, I hope that your reading turns into praying. In the remaining pages, we are all students together, going to our Lord and Teacher and asking just as his first disciples did, "Lord, teach us to pray."

Part Two

Guides for Prayer

Part Two Introduction

Guidance on Using
the Guides for Prayer

*This excellent book is fitted not for devotion only,
but instruction also...*

John Wesley

(From Wesley's introduction to *A Collection of Forms of Prayer for
Every Day of the Week*, which sought to guide readers in the same
fashion as Part Two of this book)

T he remainder of this book is designed to help
you put into practice the three ways of praying discussed
in Part One. You will find four guides for prayer for each
day of the week: morning, midday, evening, and night.
Each one will include space for praying with other
people's words, praying without words, and praying
with your own words.

Feel free to adapt your usage of these as you find best
helps you to live prayerfully. For example, although each
of these three ways of prayer is listed at every time for
prayer, I normally do not pray in all three ways at every
time of prayer. Rather, I've found that a goal which

works for me is to try to practice each way of praying for at least a few minutes each day. So, if I am able to have a time of prayer without words during morning prayer, in evening prayer I might skip that part of the guide and have a time of prayer with my own words.

In addition to experimenting with when to practice praying without words and praying with your own words, you will also want to experiment with how and how long to do so. In praying without words, five minutes at one of the prayer times each day is a good place to begin until you find yourself desiring to make it longer. Most of us will likely land somewhere between five and twenty minutes.

In praying with your own words, find a method that draws you in. It may be writing your words in a journal, or saying them aloud, or some other method that helps you to pray to God in simple ways. You can also experiment with what to do physically that most helps you to fight off those monkeys. You might want to go for a walk, sit still and breathe deeply, or find a place outside where you can see the sky or the landscape. Once you begin looking for what helps you to be prayerful, God will guide you.

There are numerous helpful published guides for prayer available in different formats. (See the "For Further Praying" section at the end of Chapter 1 for some suggestions.) My hope for including guides for prayer in this book is that they could provide a structure for allowing these three ways of praying to build on one another in your life, and that these guides might whet your appetite to make lifelong use of some of the other excellent resources available.

Each of the following guides for prayer includes some or all of the following components:

- Call to Prayer
- Psalm of Invitation
- Psalm Appropriate for the Time of Day
- Scripture Reading
- Prayer Without Words
- Response
- Prayers of the People
- The Lord's Prayer
- Prayer With Your Own Words

A common frustration for people who begin to try to learn to use a prayer guide is that they often involve a learning curve, as the person praying has to learn to turn to certain parts of the book during certain parts of the prayer. Though those habits can be learned quickly, I have tried to avoid them in these guides and make everything as simple as possible by printing everything together so that no turning back and forth between the pages is required. The only part of the prayers not printed out each time is the Lord's Prayer. Rather than printing it twenty-eight times, since it is a part of every guide included here, I have printed it once on the first page and then indicated a place within each guide when it could be prayed. If you have not committed it to memory, I think you will find it enjoyable and beneficial to do so.

I have adapted the written prayers to make them useful for individuals to pray alone and for groups to pray together. If being prayed by individuals, the communal language is a constant reminder that whenever we pray with these words of other people, we are never really doing so alone, but are joining together with Christians throughout the world today and throughout history. If being prayed by groups, one person can act as the leader and read the words in normal print and the rest of the group can say the words in bold print aloud together.

Almost nothing in these guides for prayer is original to me. Most of this is adapted from *The Book of Common Prayer*. All pieces of the content of these prayers are in the public domain, so please feel free to use anything from Part Two of this book in any way that might be helpful to you or those with whom you pray.

The Lord's Prayer

Our Father in heaven,
hallowed be your name,
your kingdom come,
your will be done,
on earth as it is in heaven.
Give us today our daily bread.
Forgive us our sins
as we forgive those
who sin against us.
Save us from the time of trial,
and deliver us from evil.
For the kingdom, the power,
and the glory are yours,
now and for ever. Amen.

Sunday
Morning Prayer

Call to Prayer

Grace to you and peace from God our Father and the Lord Jesus Christ. (Philippians 1:2)

Lord, open our lips.
And our mouth shall proclaim your praise.

The earth is the Lord's for he made it:
Come let us adore him.

Psalm of Invitation: "Christ Our Passover"

Alleluia.

Christ our Passover has been sacrificed for us; therefore let us keep the feast,

Not with the old leaven, the leaven of malice and evil, but with the unleavened bread of sincerity and truth. Alleluia.

Christ being raised from the dead will never die again; death no longer has dominion over him.

The death that he died, he died to sin, once for all; but the life he lives, he lives to God.

So also consider yourselves dead to sin,

and alive to God in Jesus Christ our Lord. **Alleluia.**

Christ has been raised from the dead,

the first fruits of those who have fallen asleep.

For since by a man came death,

by a man has come also

the resurrection of the dead.

For as in Adam all die, so also in Christ shall all be made alive. Alleluia.

(1 Corinthians 5:7-8; Romans 6:9-11;
1 Corinthians 15:20-22)

Morning Psalm

O give thanks to the Lord, for he is good;
his steadfast love endures forever!
Let Israel say,
"His steadfast love endures forever."
The Lord is my strength and my might;
he has become my salvation.
There are glad songs of victory in the tents of the
righteous:
"The right hand of the Lord does valiantly;
the right hand of the Lord is exalted;
the right hand of the Lord does valiantly."
I shall not die, but I shall live,
and recount the deeds of the Lord.
The Lord has punished me severely,
but he did not give me over to death.
Open to me the gates of righteousness,
that I may enter through them
and give thanks to the Lord.
This is the gate of the Lord;
the righteous shall enter through it.
I thank you that you have answered me
and have become my salvation.
The stone that the builders rejected
has become the chief cornerstone.
This is the Lord's doing;
it is marvelous in our eyes.
This is the day that the Lord has made;
let us rejoice and be glad in it.
(Psalm 118:1-2,14-24 NRSV)

Glory to the Father, and to the Son, and to the Holy
Spirit: as it was in the beginning, is now, and will be
for ever. Amen.

Scripture Reading

For the love of Christ urges us on, because we are convinced that one has died for all; therefore all have died. And he died for all, so that those who live might live no longer for themselves, but for him who died and was raised for them. (2 Corinthians 5:14-15, NRSV)

The Word of the Lord.
Thanks be to God.

Prayer Without Words

Response: You Are God

You are God: we praise you;
You are the Lord: we acclaim you;
You are the eternal Father:
All creation worships you.
To you all angels, all the powers of heaven,
Cherubim and Seraphim,
sing in endless praise:
Holy, holy, holy Lord,
God of power and might,
heaven and earth are full of your glory.
The glorious company of apostles praise you.
The noble fellowship of prophets praise you.
The white-robed army of martyrs praise you.
Throughout the world the holy Church acclaims you;
Father, of majesty unbounded,
your true and only Son, worthy of all worship,
and the Holy Spirit, advocate and guide.
You, Christ, are the king of glory,
the eternal Son of the Father.
When you became man to set us free
you did not shun the virgin's womb.
You overcame the sting of death

and opened the kingdom of heaven
to all believers.
You are seated at God's right hand in glory.
**We believe that you will come
and be our judge.
Come then, Lord, and help your people,
bought with the price of your own blood,
and bring us with your saints
to glory everlasting.**

Prayers of the People
The Lord be with us.
Let us pray.

The Lord's Prayer

Show us your mercy, O Lord;
And grant us your salvation.
Clothe your ministers with righteousness;
Let your people sing with joy.
Give peace, O Lord, in all the world;
For only in you can we live in safety.
Lord, keep this nation under your care;
And guide us in the way of justice and truth.
Let your way be known upon earth;
Your saving health among all nations.
Let not the needy, O Lord, be forgotten;
Nor the hope of the poor be taken away.
Create in us clean hearts, O God;
And sustain us with your Holy Spirit.

O God, you make us glad with the weekly
remembrance of the glorious resurrection of your Son
our Lord: Give us this day such blessing through our
worship of you, that the week to come may be spent in
your favor, through Jesus Christ our Lord. **Amen.**

Almighty and everlasting God, by whose Spirit the
whole body of your faithful people is governed and
sanctified: Receive our supplications and prayers
which we offer before you for all members of your holy
church, that in their vocation and ministry they may
truly and devoutly serve you; through our Lord and
Savior Jesus Christ. **Amen.**

Prayer With Your Own Words

Almighty God, Father of all mercies, we your
unworthy servants give you humble thanks
for all your goodness and loving-kindness
to us and to all whom you have made.
**We bless you for our creation, preservation,
and all the blessings of this life;**
but above all for your immeasurable love
in the redemption of the world by our Lord Jesus
Christ; for the means of grace, and for the hope of
glory.
**And, we pray,
give us such an awareness of your mercies,
that with truly thankful hearts
we may show forth your praise,
not only with our lips, but in our lives,
by giving our selves up to your service,
and by walking before you
in holiness and righteousness all our days;**

through Jesus Christ our Lord,
to whom, with you and the Holy Spirit,
be honor and glory throughout all ages. **Amen.**
(The General Thanksgiving)

Let us bless the Lord.
Thanks be to God.

The grace of the Lord Jesus Christ, and the love of God, and the fellowship of the Holy Spirit, be with us all evermore. **Amen.** (2 Corinthians 13:14)

Sunday
Midday Prayer

Call to Prayer

O God, make speed to save us.
O Lord, make haste to help us.

Midday Psalm

Your word is a lantern to my feet
and a light upon my path.
I have sworn and am determined
to keep your righteous judgments.
I am deeply troubled;
preserve my life, O Lord, according to your word.
Accept, O Lord, the willing tribute of my lips,
and teach me your judgments.
My life is always in my hand,
yet I do not forget your law.
The wicked have set a trap for me,
but I have not strayed from your commandments.
Your decrees are my inheritance for ever;
truly, they are the joy of my heart.
I have applied my heart to fulfill your statutes
for ever and to the end. (Psalm 119:105-112)

Glory to the Father, and to the Son, and to the Holy
Spirit: as it was in the beginning, is now, and will be
for ever. Amen.

Scripture Reading

The love of God has been poured into our hearts
through the Holy Spirit that has been given to us.
(Romans 5:5)

Thanks be to God.

Prayer Without Words

Prayers of the People
Lord, have mercy.
Christ, have mercy.
Lord, have mercy.

The Lord's Prayer

Lord, hear our prayer;
And let our cry come to you.
Let us pray.

Heavenly Father, send your Holy Spirit into our hearts, to direct and rule us according to your will, to comfort us in all our afflictions, to defend us from all error, and to lead us into all truth; through Jesus Christ our Lord. **Amen.**

Prayer With Your Own Words

Let us bless the Lord.
Thanks be to God.

Sunday
Evening Prayer

Call to Prayer

Let my prayer be set forth in your sight as incense, the lifting up of my hands as the evening sacrifice. (Psalm 141:2)

O God, make speed to save us.
O Lord, make haste to help us.

Evening Psalm

The Lord is my chosen portion and my cup;
you hold my lot.
The boundary lines have fallen for me in pleasant places;
I have a goodly heritage.
I bless the Lord who gives me counsel;
in the night also my heart instructs me.
I keep the Lord always before me;
because he is at my right hand, I shall not be moved.
Therefore my heart is glad, and my soul rejoices;
my body also rests secure.
For you do not give me up to Sheol,
or let your faithful one see the Pit.
You show me the path of life.
In your presence there is fullness of joy;
in your right hand are pleasures forevermore.
(Psalm 16:5-11, NRSV)

Glory to the Father, and to the Son, and to the Holy Spirit: as it was in the beginning, is now, and will be for ever. Amen.

Scripture Reading

When many of his disciples heard it, they said, "This teaching is difficult; who can accept it?" But Jesus, being aware that his disciples were complaining about it, said to them, "Does this offend you? Then what if you were to see the Son of Man ascending to where he was before? It is the spirit that gives life; the flesh is useless. The words that I have spoken to you are spirit and life. But among you there are some who do not believe." For Jesus knew from the first who were the ones that did not believe, and who was the one that would betray him. And he said, "For this reason I have told you that no one can come to me unless it is granted by the Father."

Because of this many of his disciples turned back and no longer went about with him. So Jesus asked the twelve, "Do you also wish to go away?" Simon Peter answered him, "Lord, to whom can we go? You have the words of eternal life. We have come to believe and know that you are the Holy One of God." (John 6:60-69, NRSV)

The Word of the Lord.
Thanks be to God.

Prayer Without Words

Response: The Apostles' Creed
I believe in God, the Father almighty,
creator of heaven and earth.
I believe in Jesus Christ, his only Son, our Lord.
He was conceived by the power of the Holy Spirit
and born of the Virgin Mary.
He suffered under Pontius Pilate,
was crucified, died, and was buried.

He descended to the dead.
On the third day he rose again.
He ascended into heaven,
and is seated at the right hand of the Father.
He will come again to judge the living and the
dead.
I believe in the Holy Spirit,
the holy catholic[37] church,
the forgiveness of sins,
the resurrection of the body,
and the life everlasting. Amen.

Prayers of the People

The Lord be with us.
Let us pray.

The Lord's Prayer

Show us your mercy, O Lord;
And grant us your salvation.
Clothe your ministers with righteousness;
Let your people sing with joy.
Give peace, O Lord, in all the world;
For only in you can we live in safety.
Lord, keep this nation under your care;
And guide us in the way of justice and truth.
Let your way be known upon earth;
Your saving health among all nations.
Let not the needy, O Lord, be forgotten;
Nor the hope of the poor be taken away.
Create in us clean hearts, O God;
And sustain us with your Holy Spirit.

Lord God, whose Son our Savior Jesus Christ triumphed over the powers of death and prepared for us our place in the new Jerusalem: Grant that we, who have this day given thanks for his resurrection, may praise you in that City of which he is the light, and where he lives and reigns for ever. **Amen.**

O God and Father of all, whom the whole heavens adore: Let the whole earth also worship you, all nations obey you, all tongues confess and bless you, and men and women everywhere love you and serve you in peace; through Jesus Christ our Lord. **Amen.**

Hymn of the Day: Christ the Lord is Risen Today (Charles Wesley)

Christ the Lord is risen today, Alleluia!
Earth and heaven in chorus say, Alleluia!
Raise your joys and triumphs high, Alleluia!
Sing, ye heavens, and earth reply, Alleluia!

Love's redeeming work is done, Alleluia!
Fought the fight, the battle won, Alleluia!
Death in vain forbids him rise, Alleluia!
Christ has opened paradise, Alleluia!

Lives again our glorious King, Alleluia!
Where, O death, is now thy sting? Alleluia!
Once he died our souls to save, Alleluia!
Where's thy victory, boasting grave? Alleluia!

Soar we now where Christ has led, Alleluia!
Following our exalted Head, Alleluia!
Made like him, like him we rise, Alleluia!
Ours the cross, the grave, the skies, Alleluia!

Hail the Lord of earth and heaven, Alleluia!
Praise to thee by both be given, Alleluia!
Thee we greet triumphant now, Alleluia!
Hail the Resurrection, thou, Alleluia!

King of glory, soul of bliss, Alleluia!
Everlasting life is this, Alleluia!
Thee to know, thy power to prove, Alleluia!
Thus to sing, and thus to love, Alleluia!

Prayer With Your Own Words

Almighty God, Father of all mercies, we your
unworthy servants give you humble thanks
for all your goodness and loving-kindness
to us and to all whom you have made.
**We bless you for our creation, preservation,
and all the blessings of this life;**
but above all for your immeasurable love
in the redemption of the world by our Lord Jesus
Christ; for the means of grace, and for the hope of
glory.
**And, we pray,
give us such an awareness of your mercies,
that with truly thankful hearts
we may show forth your praise,
not only with our lips, but in our lives,
by giving our selves up to your service,
and by walking before you
in holiness and righteousness all our days;**
through Jesus Christ our Lord,
to whom, with you and the Holy Spirit,
be honor and glory throughout all ages. **Amen.**
(The General Thanksgiving)

Let us bless the Lord.
Thanks be to God.

The grace of the Lord Jesus Christ, and the love of God, and the fellowship of the Holy Spirit, be with us all evermore. **Amen.** (2 Corinthians 13:14)

Sunday
Night Prayer

Call to Prayer

The Lord Almighty grant us a peaceful night and a
perfect end. **Amen.**

Our help is in the Name of the Lord;
The maker of heaven and earth.

Confession

Let us confess our sins to God.

Silence

Almighty God, our heavenly Father:
We have sinned against you,
through our own fault,
in thought, and word, and deed,
and in what we have left undone.
For the sake of your Son our Lord Jesus Christ,
forgive us all our offenses;
and grant that we may serve you
in newness of life,
to the glory of your name. Amen.

May the Almighty God
grant us forgiveness of all our sins,
and the grace and comfort of the Holy Spirit. **Amen.**

O God, make speed to save us.
O Lord, make haste to help us.

Night Psalm

Answer me when I call, O God, defender of my cause;
you set me free when I am hard-pressed;
have mercy on me and hear my prayer.

**"You mortals, how long will you dishonor my glory?
how long will you worship dumb idols
and run after false gods?"**

Know that the Lord does wonders for the faithful;
when I call upon the Lord, he will hear me.

**Tremble, then, and do not sin;
speak to your heart in silence upon your bed.**

Offer the appointed sacrifices
and put your trust in the Lord.

**Many are saying,
"Oh, that we might see better times!"
Lift up the light of your countenance upon us,
O Lord.**

You have put gladness in my heart,
more than when grain and wine and oil increase.

**I lie down in peace; at once I fall asleep;
for only you, Lord, make me dwell in safety.** (Psalm 4)

**Glory to the Father, and to the Son, and to the Holy
Spirit: as it was in the beginning, is now, and will be
for ever. Amen.**

Scripture Reading

Lord, you are in the midst of us, and we are called by
your Name: Do not forsake us, O Lord our God.
(Jeremiah 14:9,22)

Thanks be to God.

Prayer Without Words

Prayers of the People

Into your hands, O Lord, I commend my spirit;
For you have redeemed me, O Lord, O God of truth.
Keep us, O Lord, as the apple of your eye;
Hide us under the shadow of your wings.

Lord, have mercy.
Christ, have mercy.
Lord, have mercy.

The Lord's Prayer

Lord, hear our prayer;
And let our cry come to you.
Let us pray.

Be our light in the darkness, O Lord, and in your great mercy defend us from all perils and dangers of this night; for the love of your only Son, our Savior Jesus Christ. **Amen.**

Keep watch, dear Lord, with those who work, or watch, or weep this night, and give your angels charge over those who sleep. Tend the sick, Lord Christ; give rest to the weary, bless the dying, soothe the suffering, pity the afflicted, shield the joyous; and all for your love's sake. **Amen.**

Prayer With Your Own Words

Benediction
Guide us waking, O Lord, and guard us sleeping; that awake we may watch with Christ, and asleep we may rest in peace.

The Song of Simeon
Lord, you now have set your servant free
to go in peace as you have promised;
For these eyes of mine have seen the Savior,
whom you have prepared for all the world to see:
A Light to enlighten the nations,
and the glory of your people Israel. (Luke 2:29-32)

Guide us waking, O Lord, and guard us sleeping; that
awake we may watch with Christ, and asleep we may
rest in peace.

Let us bless the Lord.
Thanks be to God.

The almighty and merciful Lord, Father, Son, and Holy
Spirit, bless us and keep us. **Amen.**

Monday
Morning Prayer

Call to Prayer

I was glad when they said to me, "Let us go to the house of the Lord." (Psalm 122:1)

Lord, open our lips.
And our mouth shall proclaim your praise.

Worship the Lord in the beauty of holiness:
Come let us adore him.

Psalm of Invitation

Be joyful in the Lord, all you lands;
serve the Lord with gladness
and come before his presence with a song.
Know this: the Lord himself is God;
he himself has made us, and we are his;
we are his people and the sheep of his pasture.
Enter his gates with thanksgiving;
go into his courts with praise;
give thanks to him and call upon his Name.
For the Lord is good;
his mercy is everlasting;
and his faithfulness endures from age to age.
(Psalm 100)

Morning Psalm

Praise the Lord!
Praise God in his sanctuary;
praise him in his mighty firmament!
Praise him for his mighty deeds;
praise him according to his surpassing greatness!
Praise him with trumpet sound;
praise him with lute and harp!

Praise him with tambourine and dance;
praise him with strings and pipe!
Praise him with clanging cymbals;
praise him with loud clashing cymbals!
Let everything that breathes praise the Lord!
Praise the Lord! (Psalm 150, NRSV)

Glory to the Father, and to the Son, and to the Holy
Spirit: as it was in the beginning, is now, and will be
for ever. Amen.

Scripture Reading

"Do not let your hearts be troubled. Believe in God, believe also in me. In my Father's house there are many dwelling places. If it were not so, would I have told you that I go to prepare a place for you? And if I go and prepare a place for you, I will come again and will take you to myself, so that where I am, there you may be also. And you know the way to the place where I am going." Thomas said to him, "Lord, we do not know where you are going. How can we know the way?" Jesus said to him, "I am the way, and the truth, and the life. No one comes to the Father except through me. If you know me, you will know my Father also. From now on you do know him and have seen him." (John 14:1-7, NRSV)

The Word of the Lord.
Thanks be to God.

Prayer Without Words

Response: The Song of the Redeemed
O ruler of the universe, Lord God,
great deeds are they that you have done,
surpassing human understanding.

Your ways are ways of righteousness and truth,
O King of all the ages.
Who can fail to do you homage, Lord,
and sing the praises of your Name?
for you only are the Holy One.
All nations will draw near
and fall down before you,
because your just and holy works
have been revealed. (Revelation 15:3-4)

Prayers of the People

The Lord be with us.
Let us pray.

The Lord's Prayer

Save your people, Lord, and bless your inheritance;
Govern and uphold them, now and always.
Day by day we bless you;
We praise your Name for ever.
Lord, keep us from all sin today;
Have mercy on us, Lord, have mercy.
Lord, show us your love and mercy;
For we put our trust in you.
In you, Lord, is our hope;
And we shall never hope in vain.

O God, the King eternal, whose light divides the day
from the night and turns the shadow of death into
morning: Drive far from us all wrong desires, incline
our hearts to keep your law, and guide our feet into the
way of peace; that, having done your will with
cheerfulness during the day, we may, when night
comes, rejoice to give you thanks; through Jesus Christ
our Lord. **Amen.**

O God, you have made of one blood all the peoples of the earth, and sent your blessed Son to preach peace to those who are far off and to those who are near: Grant that people everywhere may seek after you and find you; bring all the nations into your fold; pour out your Spirit upon all flesh; and hasten the coming of your kingdom; through Jesus Christ our Lord. **Amen.**

Prayer With Your Own Words

Almighty God, you have given us grace at this time with one accord to make our common supplication to you; and you have promised through your well-beloved Son that when two or three are gathered together in his Name you will be in the midst of them: Fulfill now, O Lord, our desires and petitions as may be best for us; granting us in this world knowledge of your truth, and in the age to come life everlasting. **Amen.** (A Prayer of St. Chrysostom)

Let us bless the Lord.
Thanks be to God.

May the God of hope fill us with all joy and peace in believing through the power of the Holy Spirit. **Amen.** (Romans 15:13)

Monday
Midday Prayer

O God, make speed to save us.
O Lord, make haste to help us.

Midday Psalm

I lift up my eyes to the hills;
from where is my help to come?
My help comes from the Lord,
the maker of heaven and earth.
He will not let your foot be moved
and he who watches over you will not fall asleep.
Behold, he who keeps watch over Israel
shall neither slumber nor sleep;
The Lord himself watches over you;
the Lord is your shade at your right hand,
So that the sun shall not strike you by day,
nor the moon by night.
The Lord shall preserve you from all evil;
it is he who shall keep you safe.
The Lord shall watch over your going out
and your coming in,
from this time forth for evermore. (Psalm 121)

Glory to the Father, and to the Son, and to the Holy
Spirit: as it was in the beginning, is now, and will be
for ever. Amen.

Scripture Reading

If anyone is in Christ he is a new creation; the old has passed away, behold the new has come. All this is from God, who through Christ reconciled us to himself and gave us the ministry of reconciliation. (2 Corinthians 5:17-18)

Thanks be to God.

Prayer Without Words

Prayers of the People

Lord, have mercy.
Christ, have mercy.
Lord, have mercy.

The Lord's Prayer

Lord, hear our prayer;
And let our cry come to you.
Let us pray.

Blessed Savior, at this hour you hung upon the cross, stretching out your loving arms: Grant that all the peoples of the earth may look to you and be saved; for your tender mercies' sake. **Amen.**

Prayer With Your Own Words

Let us bless the Lord.
Thanks be to God.

Monday
Evening Prayer

Call to Prayer

Grace to you and peace from God our Father and from the Lord Jesus Christ. (Philippians 1:2)

O God, make speed to save us.
O Lord, make haste to help us.

Evening Psalm

Your steadfast love, O Lord, extends to the heavens,
your faithfulness to the clouds.
Your righteousness is like the mighty mountains,
your judgments are like the great deep;
you save humans and animals alike, O Lord.
How precious is your steadfast love, O God!
All people may take refuge in the shadow of your wings.
They feast on the abundance of your house,
and you give them drink from the river of your delights.
For with you is the fountain of life;
in your light we see light.
O continue your steadfast love to those who know you, and your salvation to the upright of heart!
(Psalm 36:5-10, NRSV)

Glory to the Father, and to the Son, and to the Holy Spirit: as it was in the beginning, is now, and will be for ever. Amen.

Scripture Reading:

There is therefore now no condemnation for those who are in Christ Jesus. For the law of the Spirit of life in Christ Jesus has set you free from the law of sin and of death. For God has done what the law, weakened by the flesh, could not do: by sending his own Son in the likeness of sinful flesh, and to deal with sin, he condemned sin in the flesh, so that the just requirement of the law might be fulfilled in us, who walk not according to the flesh but according to the Spirit. For those who live according to the flesh set their minds on the things of the flesh, but those who live according to the Spirit set their minds on the things of the Spirit. To set the mind on the flesh is death, but to set the mind on the Spirit is life and peace. (Romans 8:1-6, NRSV)

The Word of the Lord.
Thanks be to God.

Prayer Without Words

Response: The Song of Simeon

Lord, you now have set your servant free
to go in peace as you have promised;
For these eyes of mine have seen the Savior,
whom you have prepared for all the world to see:
A Light to enlighten the nations,
and the glory of your people Israel. (Luke 2:29-32)

Prayers of the People

The Lord be with us.
Let us pray.

The Lord's Prayer

That this evening may be holy, good, and peaceful,
we entreat you, O Lord.
That your holy angels may lead us in paths of peace
and goodwill, **we entreat you, O Lord.**
That we may be pardoned and forgiven for our sins
and offenses, **we entreat you, O Lord.**
That there may be peace to your Church and to the
whole world, **we entreat you, O Lord.**
That we may depart this life in your faith and fear, and
not be condemned before the great judgment seat of
Christ, **we entreat you, O Lord.**
That we may be bound together by your Holy Spirit in
the communion of [_____ and] all your saints,
entrusting one another and all our life to Christ,
we entreat you, O Lord.

Most holy God, the source of all good desires, all right
judgments, and all just works: Give to us, your
servants, that peace which the world cannot give, so
that our minds may be fixed on the doing of your will,
and that we, being delivered from the fear of all
enemies, may live in peace and quietness; through the
mercies of Christ Jesus our Savior. **Amen.**

Keep watch, dear Lord, with those who work, or
watch, or weep this night, and give your angels charge
over those who sleep. Tend the sick, Lord Christ; give
rest to the weary, bless the dying, soothe the suffering,
pity the afflicted, shield the joyous; and all for your
love's sake. **Amen.**

Evening Hymn: O For a Thousand Tongues to Sing
(Charles Wesley)

O for a thousand tongues to sing
my great Redeemer's praise,
the glories of my God and King,
the triumphs of his grace!

My gracious Master and my God,
assist me to proclaim,
to spread through all the earth abroad
the honors of thy name.

Jesus! the name that charms our fears,
that bids our sorrows cease;
'tis music in the sinner's ears,
'tis life, and health, and peace.

He breaks the power of canceled sin,
he sets the prisoner free;
his blood can make the foulest clean;
his blood availed for me.

He speaks, and listening to his voice,
new life the dead receive;
the mournful, broken hearts rejoice,
the humble poor believe.

Hear him, ye deaf; his praise, ye dumb,
your loosened tongues employ;
ye blind, behold your savior come,
and leap, ye lame, for joy.

In Christ, your head, you then shall know,
shall feel your sins forgiven;
anticipate your heaven below,
and own that love is heaven.

Prayer With Your Own Words

Almighty God, you have given us grace at this time
with one accord to make our common supplication to
you; and you have promised through your well-
beloved Son that when two or three are gathered
together in his Name you will be in the midst of them:
Fulfill now, O Lord, our desires and petitions as may
be best for us; granting us in this world knowledge of
your truth, and in the age to come life everlasting.
Amen. *(A Prayer of St. Chrysostom)*

Let us bless the Lord.
Thanks be to God.

May the God of hope fill us with all joy and peace in
believing through the power of the Holy Spirit. **Amen.**
(Romans 15:13)

Monday
Night Prayer

Call to Prayer

The Lord Almighty grant us a peaceful night and a perfect end. **Amen.**

Our help is in the Name of the Lord;
The maker of heaven and earth.

Confession

Let us confess our sins to God.

Silence

Almighty God, our heavenly Father:
We have sinned against you,
through our own fault,
in thought, and word, and deed,
and in what we have left undone.
For the sake of your Son our Lord Jesus Christ,
forgive us all our offenses;
and grant that we may serve you
in newness of life,
to the glory of your name. Amen.

May the Almighty God
grant us forgiveness of all our sins,
and the grace and comfort of the Holy Spirit. **Amen.**

O God, make speed to save us.
O Lord, make haste to help us.

Night Psalm

In you, O Lord, have I taken refuge;
let me never be put to shame:
deliver me in your righteousness.
Incline your ear to me;
make haste to deliver me.
Be my strong rock, a castle to keep me safe,
for you are my crag and my stronghold;
for the sake of your Name, lead me and guide me.
Take me out of the net that they have secretly set for me,
for you are my tower of strength.
Into your hands I commend my spirit,
for you have redeemed me,
O Lord, O God of truth. (Psalm 31)

Glory to the Father, and to the Son, and to the Holy Spirit: as it was in the beginning, is now, and will be for ever. Amen.

Scripture Reading

Come to me, all who labor and are heavy-laden, and I will give you rest. Take my yoke upon you, and learn from me; for I am gentle and lowly in heart, and you will find rest for your souls. For my yoke is easy, and my burden is light. (Matthew 11:28-30)

Thanks be to God.

Prayer Without Words

Prayers of the People

Into your hands, O Lord, I commend my spirit;
For you have redeemed me, O Lord, O God of truth.
Keep us, O Lord, as the apple of your eye;
Hide us under the shadow of your wings.

Lord, have mercy.
Christ, have mercy.
Lord, have mercy.

The Lord's Prayer

Lord, hear our prayer;
And let our cry come to you.
Let us pray.

Be present, O merciful God, and protect us through the hours of this night, so that we who are wearied by the changes and chances of this life may rest in your eternal changelessness; through Jesus Christ our Lord. **Amen.**

O God, your unfailing providence sustains both the world we live in and the life we live: Watch over those, both night and day, who work while others sleep, and grant that we may never forget that our common life depends upon each other's toil; through Jesus Christ our Lord. **Amen.**

Prayer With Your Own Words

Benediction

Guide us waking, O Lord, and guard us sleeping; that awake we may watch with Christ, and asleep we may rest in peace.

The Song of Simeon

Lord, you now have set your servant free
to go in peace as you have promised;
**For these eyes of mine have seen the Savior,
whom you have prepared for all the world to see:**

A Light to enlighten the nations,
and the glory of your people Israel. (Luke 2:29-32)

Guide us waking, O Lord, and guard us sleeping; that awake we may watch with Christ, and asleep we may rest in peace.

Let us bless the Lord.
Thanks be to God.

The almighty and merciful Lord, Father, Son, and Holy Spirit, bless us and keep us. **Amen.**

Tuesday
Morning Prayer

Let the words of my mouth and the meditation of my heart be acceptable in your sight, O Lord, my strength and my redeemer. (Psalm 19:14)

Lord, open our lips.
And our mouth shall proclaim your praise.

The mercy of the Lord is everlasting:
Come let us adore him.

Psalm of Invitation

Come, let us sing to the Lord.
Let us shout for joy to the Rock of our salvation.
Let us come before his presence with thanksgiving and raise a loud shout to him with psalms.
For the Lord is a great God,
and a great King above all gods.
In his hand are the caverns of the earth, and the heights of the hills are his also.
The sea is his, for he made it,
and his hands have molded the dry land.
Come, let us bow down, and bend the knee, and kneel before the Lord our Maker.
For he is our God,
and we are the people of his pasture
and the sheep of his hand.
Oh, that today you would hearken to his voice!
(Psalm 95:1-7)

Morning Psalm

The Lord is gracious and merciful,
slow to anger and abounding in steadfast love.
The Lord is good to all,
and his compassion is over all that he has made.
All your works shall give thanks to you, O Lord,
and all your faithful shall bless you.
They shall speak of the glory of your kingdom,
and tell of your power,
to make known to all people your mighty deeds,
and the glorious splendor of your kingdom.
Your kingdom is an everlasting kingdom,
and your dominion endures throughout all
generations.
The Lord is faithful in all his words,
and gracious in all his deeds.
The Lord upholds all who are falling,
and raises up all who are bowed down.
The eyes of all look to you,
and you give them their food in due season.
You open your hand,
satisfying the desire of every living thing.
The Lord is just in all his ways,
and kind in all his doings.
The Lord is near to all who call on him,
to all who call on him in truth.
He fulfills the desire of all who fear him;
he also hears their cry, and saves them.
The Lord watches over all who love him,
but all the wicked he will destroy.
My mouth will speak the praise of the Lord,
and all flesh will bless his holy name forever and
ever. (Psalm 145:8-21, NRSV)

Glory to the Father, and to the Son, and to the Holy Spirit: as it was in the beginning, is now, and will be for ever. Amen.

Scripture Reading

For this very reason, you must make every effort to support your faith with goodness, and goodness with knowledge, and knowledge with self-control, and self-control with endurance, and endurance with godliness, and godliness with mutual affection, and mutual affection with love. For if these things are yours and are increasing among you, they keep you from being ineffective and unfruitful in the knowledge of our Lord Jesus Christ. For anyone who lacks these things is nearsighted and blind, and is forgetful of the cleansing of past sins.

(2 Peter 1:5-9, NRSV)

The Word of the Lord.
Thanks be to God.

Prayer Without Words

Response: A Song to the Lamb

Splendor and honor and kingly power
are yours by right, O Lord our God,
For you created everything that is,
and by your will they were created and have their being;
And yours by right, O Lamb that was slain,
for with your blood you have redeemed for God,
from every family, language, people, and nation, a kingdom of priests to serve our God.

And so, to him who sits upon the throne,
and to Christ the Lamb, be worship and praise,
dominion and splendor, for ever and for evermore.
(Revelation 4:11, 5:9-10,13)

Prayers of the People
The Lord be with us.
Let us pray.

The Lord's Prayer

Show us your mercy, O Lord;
And grant us your salvation.
Clothe your ministers with righteousness;
Let your people sing with joy.
Give peace, O Lord, in all the world;
For only in you can we live in safety.
Lord, keep this nation under your care;
And guide us in the way of justice and truth.
Let your way be known upon earth;
Your saving health among all nations.
Let not the needy, O Lord, be forgotten;
Nor the hope of the poor be taken away.
Create in us clean hearts, O God;
And sustain us with your Holy Spirit.

O God, the author of peace and lover of concord, to
know you is eternal life and to serve you is perfect
freedom: Defend us, your humble servants, in all
assaults of our enemies; that we, surely trusting in your
defense, may not fear the power of any adversaries;
through the might of Jesus Christ our Lord. **Amen.**

Lord Jesus Christ, you stretched out your arms of love on the hard wood of the cross that everyone might come within the reach of your saving embrace: So clothe us in your Spirit that we, reaching forth our hands in love, may bring those who do not know you to the knowledge and love of your Name. **Amen.**

Prayer With Your Own Words

Almighty God, Father of all mercies, we your unworthy servants give you humble thanks for all your goodness and loving-kindness to us and to all whom you have made.
We bless you for our creation, preservation, and all the blessings of this life;
but above all for your immeasurable love in the redemption of the world by our Lord Jesus Christ; for the means of grace, and for the hope of glory.
And, we pray,
give us such an awareness of your mercies,
that with truly thankful hearts
we may show forth your praise,
not only with our lips, but in our lives,
by giving our selves up to your service,
and by walking before you
in holiness and righteousness all our days;
through Jesus Christ our Lord,
to whom, with you and the Holy Spirit,
be honor and glory throughout all ages. **Amen.**
(The General Thanksgiving)

Let us bless the Lord.
Thanks be to God.

Glory to God, whose power, working in us, can do infinitely more than we can ask or imagine: Glory to him from generation to generation in the Church, and in Christ Jesus for ever and ever. **Amen.** (Ephesians 3:20-21)

Tuesday
Midday Prayer

Call to Prayer

O God, make speed to save us.
O Lord, make haste to help us.

Midday Psalm

When the Lord restored the fortunes of Zion,
then were we like those who dream.
Then was our mouth filled with laughter,
and our tongue with shouts of joy.
Then they said among the nations,
"The Lord has done great things for them."
The Lord has done great things for us,
and we are glad indeed.
Restore our fortunes, O Lord,
like the watercourses of the Negev.
Those who sowed with tears
will reap with songs of joy.
Those who go out weeping, carrying the seed,
will come again with joy, shouldering their sheaves.
(Psalm 126)

Glory to the Father, and to the Son, and to the Holy
Spirit: as it was in the beginning, is now, and will be
for ever. Amen.

Scripture Reading

From the rising of the sun to its setting my Name shall be great among the nations, and in every place incense shall be offered to my Name, and a pure offering; for my Name shall be great among the nations, says the Lord of Hosts. (Malachi 1:11)

Thanks be to God.

Prayer Without Words

Prayers of the People

Lord, have mercy.
Christ, have mercy.
Lord, have mercy.

The Lord's Prayer

Lord, hear our prayer;
And let our cry come to you.
Let us pray.

Almighty Savior, who at noonday called your servant Saint Paul to be an apostle to the Gentiles: We pray you to illumine the world with the radiance of your glory, that all nations may come and worship you; for you live and reign for ever and ever. **Amen.**

Prayer With Your Own Words

Let us bless the Lord.
Thanks be to God.

Tuesday
Evening Prayer

Worship the Lord in the beauty of holiness; let the whole earth tremble before him. (Psalm 96:9)

O God, make speed to save us.
O Lord, make haste to help us.

Evening Psalm

O God, you are my God, I seek you, my soul thirsts for you; my flesh faints for you,
as in a dry and weary land where there is no water.
So I have looked upon you in the sanctuary,
beholding your power and glory.
Because your steadfast love is better than life,
my lips will praise you.
So I will bless you as long as I live;
I will lift up my hands and call on your name.
My soul is satisfied as with a rich feast,
and my mouth praises you with joyful lips
when I think of you on my bed,
and meditate on you in the watches of the night;
for you have been my help,
and in the shadow of your wings I sing for joy.
My soul clings to you;
your right hand upholds me. (Psalm 63:1-8, NRSV)

Glory to the Father, and to the Son, and to the Holy Spirit: as it was in the beginning, is now, and will be for ever. Amen.

Scripture Reading

Therefore I tell you, do not worry about your life, what you will eat or what you will drink, or about your body, what you will wear. Is not life more than food, and the body more than clothing? Look at the birds of the air; they neither sow nor reap nor gather into barns, and yet your heavenly Father feeds them. Are you not of more value than they? And can any of you by worrying add a single hour to your span of life? And why do you worry about clothing? Consider the lilies of the field, how they grow; they neither toil nor spin, yet I tell you, even Solomon in all his glory was not clothed like one of these. But if God so clothes the grass of the field, which is alive today and tomorrow is thrown into the oven, will he not much more clothe you—you of little faith? Therefore do not worry, saying, "What will we eat?" or "What will we drink?" or "What will we wear?" For it is the Gentiles who strive for all these things; and indeed your heavenly Father knows that you need all these things. But strive first for the kingdom of God and his righteousness, and all these things will be given to you as well.

So do not worry about tomorrow, for tomorrow will bring worries of its own. Today's trouble is enough for today. (Matthew 6:25-34, NRSV)

The Word of the Lord.
Thanks be to God.

Prayer Without Words

Response: *The Song of Mary*

My soul proclaims the greatness of the Lord,
my spirit rejoices in God my Savior;
for he has looked with favor on his lowly servant.
From this day all generations will call me blessed:
the Almighty has done great things for me,
and holy is his Name.
He has mercy on those who fear him
in every generation.
He has shown the strength of his arm,
he has scattered the proud in their conceit.
He has cast down the mighty from their thrones,
and has lifted up the lowly.
He has filled the hungry with good things,
and the rich he has sent away empty.
He has come to the help of his servant Israel,
for he has remembered his promise of mercy,
The promise he made to our fathers,
to Abraham and his children for ever. (Luke 1:46-55)

Prayers of the People

The Lord be with us.
Let us pray.

The Lord's Prayer

Show us your mercy, O Lord;
And grant us your salvation.
Clothe your ministers with righteousness;
Let your people sing with joy.
Give peace, O Lord, in all the world;
For only in you can we live in safety.
Lord, keep this nation under your care;
And guide us in the way of justice and truth.

Let your way be known upon earth;
Your saving health among all nations.
Let not the needy, O Lord, be forgotten;
Nor the hope of the poor be taken away.
Create in us clean hearts, O God;
And sustain us with your Holy Spirit.

Be our light in the darkness, O Lord, and in your great mercy defend us from all perils and dangers of this night; for the love of your only Son, our Savior Jesus Christ. **Amen.**

O God, you manifest in your servants the signs of your presence: Send forth upon us the Spirit of love, that in companionship with one another your abounding grace may increase among us; through Jesus Christ our Lord. **Amen.**

Hymn of the Day: And Can it Be that I Should Gain (Charles Wesley)

And can it be that I should gain
an interest in the Savior's blood!
Died he for me? who caused his pain!
For me? who him to death pursued?
Amazing love! How can it be
that thou, my God, shouldst die for me?

He left his Father's throne above
(so free, so infinite his grace!),
emptied himself of all but love,
and bled for Adam's helpless race.
'Tis mercy all, immense and free,
for O my God, it found out me!

Long my imprisoned spirit lay,
fast bound in sin and nature's night;
thine eye diffused a quickening ray;
I woke, the dungeon flamed with light;
my chains fell off, my heart was free,
I rose, went forth, and followed thee.

No condemnation now I dread;
Jesus, and all in him, is mine;
alive in him, my living Head,
and clothed in righteousness divine,
bold I approach th' eternal throne,
and claim the crown, through Christ my own.

Prayer With Your Own Words

Almighty God, Father of all mercies, we your
unworthy servants give you humble thanks
for all your goodness and loving-kindness
to us and to all whom you have made.
**We bless you for our creation, preservation,
and all the blessings of this life;**
but above all for your immeasurable love
in the redemption of the world by our Lord Jesus
Christ; for the means of grace, and for the hope of
glory.
**And, we pray,
give us such an awareness of your mercies,
that with truly thankful hearts
we may show forth your praise,
not only with our lips, but in our lives,
by giving our selves up to your service,
and by walking before you
in holiness and righteousness all our days;**

through Jesus Christ our Lord,
to whom, with you and the Holy Spirit,
be honor and glory throughout all ages. **Amen.**
(The General Thanksgiving)

Let us bless the Lord.
Thanks be to God.

Glory to God whose power, working in us, can do
infinitely more than we can ask or imagine: Glory to him
from generation to generation in the Church, and in
Christ Jesus for ever and ever. **Amen.** (Ephesians 3:20-21)

Tuesday
Night Prayer

The Lord Almighty grant us a peaceful night and a perfect end. **Amen.**

Our help is in the Name of the Lord;
The maker of heaven and earth.

Confession
Let us confess our sins to God.

Silence

Almighty God, our heavenly Father:
We have sinned against you,
through our own fault,
in thought, and word, and deed,
and in what we have left undone.
For the sake of your Son our Lord Jesus Christ,
forgive us all our offenses;
and grant that we may serve you
in newness of life,
to the glory of your name. Amen.

May the Almighty God
grant us forgiveness of all our sins,
and the grace and comfort of the Holy Spirit. **Amen.**

O God, make speed to save us.
O Lord, make haste to help us.

Night Psalm
He who dwells in the shelter of the Most High
abides under the shadow of the Almighty.
He shall say to the Lord,

"You are my refuge and my stronghold,
my God in whom I put my trust."
He shall deliver you from the snare of the hunter
and from the deadly pestilence.
He shall cover you with his pinions,
and you shall find refuge under his wings;
his faithfulness shall be a shield and a buckler.
You shall not be afraid of any terror by night,
nor of the arrow that flies by day;
Of the plague that stalks in the darkness,
nor of the sickness that lays waste at mid-day.
A thousand shall fall at your side
and ten thousand at your right hand,
but it shall not come near you.
Your eyes have only to behold
to see the reward of the wicked.
Because you have made the Lord your refuge,
and the Most High your habitation,
There shall no evil happen to you,
neither shall any plague come near your dwelling.
For he shall give his angels charge over you,
to keep you in all your ways.
They shall bear you in their hands,
lest you dash your foot against a stone.
You shall tread upon the lion and the adder;
you shall trample the young lion and the serpent
under your feet.
Because he is bound to me in love,
therefore will I deliver him;
I will protect him, because he knows my Name.
He shall call upon me, and I will answer him;
I am with him in trouble;
I will rescue him and bring him to honor.

**With long life will I satisfy him,
and show him my salvation.** (Psalm 91)

**Glory to the Father, and to the Son, and to the Holy
Spirit: as it was in the beginning, is now, and will be
for ever. Amen.**

Scripture Reading

May the God of peace, who brought again from the
dead our Lord Jesus, the great shepherd of the sheep,
by the blood of the eternal covenant, equip you with
everything good that you may do his will, working in
you that which is pleasing in his sight; through Jesus
Christ, to whom be glory for ever and ever.
(Hebrews 13:20-21)

Thanks be to God.

Prayer Without Words

Prayers of the People

Into your hands, O Lord, I commend my spirit;
For you have redeemed me, O Lord, O God of truth.
Keep us, O Lord, as the apple of your eye;
Hide us under the shadow of your wings.

Lord, have mercy.
Christ, have mercy.
Lord, have mercy.

The Lord's Prayer

Lord, hear our prayer;
And let our cry come to you.
Let us pray.

Look down, O Lord, from your heavenly throne, and
illumine this night with your celestial brightness; that

by night as by day your people may glorify your holy Name; through Jesus Christ our Lord. **Amen.**

Keep watch, dear Lord, with those who work, or watch, or weep this night, and give your angels charge over those who sleep. Tend the sick, Lord Christ; give rest to the weary, bless the dying, soothe the suffering, pity the afflicted, shield the joyous; and all for your love's sake. **Amen.**

Prayer With Your Own Words

Benediction

Guide us waking, O Lord, and guard us sleeping; that awake we may watch with Christ, and asleep we may rest in peace.

The Song of Simeon

Lord, you now have set your servant free
to go in peace as you have promised;
For these eyes of mine have seen the Savior,
whom you have prepared for all the world to see:
A Light to enlighten the nations,
and the glory of your people Israel. (Luke 2:29-32)

Guide us waking, O Lord, and guard us sleeping; that awake we may watch with Christ, and asleep we may rest in peace.

Let us bless the Lord.
Thanks be to God.

The almighty and merciful Lord, Father, Son, and Holy Spirit, bless us and keep us. **Amen.**

Wednesday
Morning Prayer

Call to Prayer
Send out your light and your truth, that they may lead me, and bring me to your holy hill and to your dwelling. (Psalm 43:3)

Lord, open our lips.
And our mouth shall proclaim your praise.

The earth is the Lord's for he made it:
Come let us adore him.

Psalm of Invitation
Be joyful in the Lord, all you lands;
serve the Lord with gladness
and come before his presence with a song.
Know this: the Lord himself is God;
he himself has made us, and we are his;
we are his people and the sheep of his pasture.
Enter his gates with thanksgiving;
go into his courts with praise;
give thanks to him and call upon his Name.
For the Lord is good;
his mercy is everlasting;
and his faithfulness endures from age to age.
(Psalm 100)

Morning Psalm
O Lord, our Sovereign,
how majestic is your name in all the earth!
You have set your glory above the heavens.
Out of the mouths of babes and infants
you have founded a bulwark because of your foes,
to silence the enemy and the avenger.

When I look at your heavens, the work of your fingers,
the moon and the stars that you have established;
what are human beings that you are mindful of them,
mortals that you care for them?
Yet you have made them a little lower than God,
and crowned them with glory and honor.
You have given them dominion over the works of
your hands;
you have put all things under their feet,
all sheep and oxen,
and also the beasts of the field,
the birds of the air, and the fish of the sea,
whatever passes along the paths of the seas.
O Lord, our Sovereign,
how majestic is your name in all the earth!
(Psalm 8, NRSV)

Glory to the Father, and to the Son, and to the Holy
Spirit: as it was in the beginning, is now, and will be
for ever. Amen.

Scripture Reading

He called the crowd with his disciples, and said to
them, "If any want to become my followers, let them
deny themselves and take up their cross and follow
me. For those who want to save their life will lose it,
and those who lose their life for my sake, and for the
sake of the gospel, will save it. For what will it profit
them to gain the whole world and forfeit their life?
(Mark 8:34-36, NRSV)

The Word of the Lord.
Thanks be to God.

Prayer Without Words

Response: *The Song of Zechariah*

Blessed be the Lord, the God of Israel;
he has come to his people and set them free.
He has raised up for us a mighty savior,
born of the house of his servant David.
Through his holy prophets he promised of old,
that he would save us from our enemies,
from the hands of all who hate us.
He promised to show mercy to our fathers
and to remember his holy covenant.
This was the oath he swore to our father Abraham,
to set us free from the hands of our enemies,
Free to worship him without fear,
holy and righteous in his sight
all the days of our life.
You, my child, shall be called
prophet of the Most High,
for you will go before the Lord to prepare his way,
to give his people knowledge of salvation
by the forgiveness of their sins.
In the tender compassion of our God
the dawn from on high shall break upon us,
To shine on those who dwell in darkness and the
shadow of death,
and guide our feet into the way of peace.
(Luke 1:68-79)

Prayers of the People

The Lord be with us.
Let us pray.

The Lord's Prayer

Save your people, Lord, and bless your inheritance;
Govern and uphold them, now and always.

Day by day we bless you;
We praise your Name for ever.
Lord, keep us from all sin today;
Have mercy on us, Lord, have mercy.
Lord, show us your love and mercy;
For we put our trust in you.
In you, Lord, is our hope;
And we shall never hope in vain.

Lord God, almighty and everlasting Father, you have brought us in safety to this new day: Preserve us with your mighty power, that we may not fall into sin, nor be overcome by adversity; and in all we do, direct us to the fulfilling of your purpose; through Jesus Christ our Lord. **Amen.**

Almighty and everlasting God, by whose Spirit the whole body of your faithful people is governed and sanctified: Receive our supplications and prayers which we offer before you for all members of your holy Church, that in their vocation and ministry they may truly and devoutly serve you; through our Lord and Savior Jesus Christ. **Amen.**

Prayer With Your Own Words

Almighty God, you have given us grace at this time with one accord to make our common supplication to you; and you have promised through your well-beloved Son that when two or three are gathered together in his Name you will be in the midst of them: Fulfill now, O Lord, our desires and petitions as may be best for us; granting us in this world knowledge of your truth, and in the age to come life everlasting. **Amen.** (A Prayer of St. Chrysostom)

Let us bless the Lord.
Thanks be to God.

The grace of our Lord Jesus Christ, and the love of God, and the fellowship of the Holy Spirit, be with us all evermore. **Amen.** (2 Corinthians 13:14)

Wednesday
Midday Prayer

Call to Prayer

O God, make speed to save us.
O Lord, make haste to help us.

Midday Psalm

Your word is a lantern to my feet
and a light upon my path.
I have sworn and am determined
to keep your righteous judgments.
I am deeply troubled;
preserve my life, O Lord, according to your word.
Accept, O Lord, the willing tribute of my lips,
and teach me your judgments.
My life is always in my hand,
yet I do not forget your law.
The wicked have set a trap for me,
but I have not strayed from your commandments.
Your decrees are my inheritance for ever;
truly, they are the joy of my heart.
I have applied my heart to fulfill your statutes
for ever and to the end. (Psalm 119:105-112)

Glory to the Father, and to the Son, and to the Holy
Spirit: as it was in the beginning, is now, and will be
for ever. Amen.

Scripture Reading

The love of God has been poured into our hearts
through the Holy Spirit that has been given to us.
(Romans 5:5)

Thanks be to God.

Prayer Without Words

Prayers of the People
Lord, have mercy.
Christ, have mercy.
Lord, have mercy.

The Lord's Prayer

Lord, hear our prayer;
And let our cry come to you.
Let us pray.

Lord Jesus Christ, you said to your apostles, "Peace I give to you; my own peace I leave with you:" Regard not our sins, but the faith of your Church, and give to us the peace and unity of that heavenly City, where with the Father and the Holy Spirit you live and reign, now and forever. **Amen.**

Prayer With Your Own Words

Let us bless the Lord.
Thanks be to God.

Wednesday
Evening Prayer

Yours is the day, O God, yours also the night; you established the moon and the sun. You fixed all the boundaries of the earth; you made both summer and winter. (Psalm 74:15-16)

O God, make speed to save us.
O Lord, make haste to help us.

Evening Psalm:

Be pleased, O God, to deliver me.
O Lord, make haste to help me!
Let those be put to shame and confusion
who seek my life.
Let those be turned back and brought to dishonor
who desire to hurt me.
Let those who say, "Aha, Aha!"
turn back because of their shame.
Let all who seek you
rejoice and be glad in you.
Let those who love your salvation
say evermore, "God is great!"
But I am poor and needy;
hasten to me, O God!
You are my help and my deliverer;
O Lord, do not delay! (Psalm 70, NRSV)

Glory to the Father, and to the Son, and to the Holy Spirit: as it was in the beginning, is now, and will be for ever. Amen.

Scripture Reading

Let love be genuine; hate what is evil, hold fast to what is good; love one another with mutual affection; outdo one another in showing honor. Do not lag in zeal, be ardent in spirit, serve the Lord. Rejoice in hope, be patient in suffering, persevere in prayer. Contribute to the needs of the saints; extend hospitality to strangers. (Romans 12:9-13, NRSV)

The Word of the Lord.
Thanks be to God.

Prayer Without Words

Response: The Song of Simeon
Lord, you now have set your servant free
to go in peace as you have promised;
For these eyes of mine have seen the Savior,
whom you have prepared for all the world to see:
A Light to enlighten the nations,
and the glory of your people Israel. (Luke 2:29-32)

Prayers of the People

The Lord be with us.
Let us pray.

The Lord's Prayer

That this evening may be holy, good, and peaceful,
we entreat you, O Lord.
That your holy angels may lead us in paths of peace and goodwill, **we entreat you, O Lord.**
That we may be pardoned and forgiven for our sins and offenses, **we entreat you, O Lord.**
That there may be peace to your Church and to the whole world, **we entreat you, O Lord.**

That we may depart this life in your faith and fear, and not be condemned before the great judgment seat of Christ, **we entreat you, O Lord.**

That we may be bound together by your Holy Spirit in the communion of [_____ and] all your saints, entrusting one another and all our life to Christ, **we entreat you, O Lord.**

O God, the life of all who live, the light of the faithful, the strength of those who labor, and the repose of the dead: We thank you for the blessings of the day that is past, and humbly ask for your protection through the coming night. Bring us in safety to the morning hours; through him who died and rose again for us, your Son our Savior Jesus Christ. **Amen.**

O God and Father of all, whom the whole heavens adore: Let the whole earth also worship you, all nations obey you, all tongues confess and bless you, and men and women everywhere love you and serve you in peace; through Jesus Christ our Lord. **Amen.**

Hymn of the Day: Phos Hilaron

O gracious Light, pure brightness of the everliving Father in heaven,
O Jesus Christ, holy and blessed!
Now as we come to the setting of the sun,
and our eyes behold the vesper light,
we sing your praises, O God:
Father, Son, and Holy Spirit.
You are worthy at all times to be praised by happy voices, O Son of God, O Giver of life, and to be glorified through all the worlds.

Prayer With Your Own Words

Almighty God, you have given us grace at this time with one accord to make our common supplication to you; and you have promised through your well-beloved Son that when two or three are gathered together in his Name you will be in the midst of them: Fulfill now, O Lord, our desires and petitions as may be best for us; granting us in this world knowledge of your truth, and in the age to come life everlasting. **Amen.** (A Prayer of St. Chrysostom)

Let us bless the Lord.
Thanks be to God.

The grace of our Lord Jesus Christ, and the love of God, and the fellowship of the Holy Spirit, be with us all evermore. **Amen.** (2 Corinthians 13:14)

Wednesday
Night Prayer

The Lord Almighty grant us a peaceful night and a
perfect end. **Amen.**

Our help is in the Name of the Lord;
The maker of heaven and earth.

Confession

Let us confess our sins to God.

Silence

Almighty God, our heavenly Father:
We have sinned against you,
through our own fault,
in thought, and word, and deed,
and in what we have left undone.
For the sake of your Son our Lord Jesus Christ,
forgive us all our offenses;
and grant that we may serve you
in newness of life,
to the glory of your name. Amen.

May the Almighty God
grant us forgiveness of all our sins,
and the grace and comfort of the Holy Spirit. **Amen.**

O God, make speed to save us.
O Lord, make haste to help us.

Night Psalm

Come, bless the Lord, all you servants of the Lord, who stand by night in the house of the Lord!
Lift up your hands to the holy place, and bless the Lord.
May the Lord, maker of heaven and earth, bless you from Zion. (Psalm 134)

Glory to the Father, and to the Son, and to the Holy Spirit: as it was in the beginning, is now, and will be for ever. Amen.

Scripture Reading

Be sober, be watchful. Your adversary the devil prowls around like a roaring lion, seeking someone to devour. Resist him, firm in your faith. (1 Peter 5:8-9a)

Thanks be to God.

Prayer Without Words

Prayers of the People

Into your hands, O Lord, I commend my spirit;
For you have redeemed me, O Lord, O God of truth.
Keep us, O Lord, as the apple of your eye;
Hide us under the shadow of your wings.

Lord, have mercy.
Christ, have mercy.
Lord, have mercy.

The Lord's Prayer

Lord, hear our prayer;
And let our cry come to you.
Let us pray.

Visit this place, O Lord, and drive far from it all snares of the enemy; let your holy angels dwell with us to preserve us in peace; and let your blessings be upon us always; through Jesus Christ our Lord. **Amen.**

O God, your unfailing providence sustains both the world we live in and the life we live: Watch over those, both night and day, who work while others sleep, and grant that we may never forget that our common life depends upon each other's toil; through Jesus Christ our Lord. **Amen.**

Prayer With Your Own Words

Benediction

Guide us waking, O Lord, and guard us sleeping; that awake we may watch with Christ, and asleep we may rest in peace.

The Song of Simeon

Lord, you now have set your servant free
to go in peace as you have promised;
For these eyes of mine have seen the Savior,
whom you have prepared for all the world to see:
A Light to enlighten the nations,
and the glory of your people Israel. (Luke 2:29-32)

Guide us waking, O Lord, and guard us sleeping; that awake we may watch with Christ, and asleep we may rest in peace.

Let us bless the Lord.
Thanks be to God.

The almighty and merciful Lord, Father, Son, and Holy Spirit, bless us and keep us. **Amen.**

Thursday
Morning Prayer

Call to Prayer
The Lord is in his holy temple; let all the earth keep
silence before him. (Habakkuk 2:20)

Lord, open our lips.
And our mouth shall proclaim your praise.

Worship the Lord in the beauty of holiness: **Come let
us adore him.**

Psalm of Invitation
Come, let us sing to the Lord.
Let us shout for joy to the Rock of our salvation.
**Let us come before his presence with thanksgiving
and raise a loud shout to him with psalms.**
For the Lord is a great God,
and a great King above all gods.
**In his hand are the caverns of the earth,
and the heights of the hills are his also.**
The sea is his, for he made it,
and his hands have molded the dry land.
**Come, let us bow down, and bend the knee,
and kneel before the Lord our Maker.**
For he is our God,
and we are the people of his pasture
and the sheep of his hand.
Oh, that today you would hearken to his voice!
(Psalm 95:1-7)

Morning Psalm
For God alone my soul waits in silence,
for my hope is from him.
He alone is my rock and my salvation,

my fortress; I shall not be shaken.
On God rests my deliverance and my honor;
my mighty rock, my refuge is in God.
Trust in him at all times, O people;
pour out your heart before him;
God is a refuge for us.
Those of low estate are but a breath,
those of high estate are a delusion;
in the balances they go up;
they are together lighter than a breath.
Put no confidence in extortion,
and set no vain hopes on robbery;
if riches increase, do not set your heart on them.
Once God has spoken;
twice have I heard this:
that power belongs to God,
and steadfast love belongs to you, O Lord.
For you repay to all according to their work.
(Psalm 62:5-12, NRSV)

Glory to the Father, and to the Son, and to the Holy
Spirit: as it was in the beginning, is now, and will be
for ever. Amen.

Scripture Reading

I appeal to you therefore, brothers and sisters, by the
mercies of God, to present your bodies as a living
sacrifice, holy and acceptable to God, which is your
spiritual worship. Do not be conformed to this world,
but be transformed by the renewing of your minds, so
that you may discern what is the will of God—what is
good and acceptable and perfect.
(Romans 12:1-2, NRSV)

The Word of the Lord.
Thanks be to God.

Prayer Without Words

Response: Glory to God
Glory to God in the highest,
and peace to his people on earth.
Lord God, heavenly King,
almighty God and Father,
we worship you, we give you thanks,
we praise you for your glory.
Lord Jesus Christ, only Son of the Father,
Lord God, Lamb of God,
you take away the sin of the world:
have mercy on us;
you are seated at the right hand of the Father:
receive our prayer.
For you alone are the Holy One,
you alone are the Lord,
you alone are the Most High,
Jesus Christ,
with the Holy Spirit,
in the glory of God the Father. Amen.

Prayers of the People
The Lord be with us.
Let us pray.

The Lord's Prayer

Show us your mercy, O Lord;
And grant us your salvation.
Clothe your ministers with righteousness;
Let your people sing with joy.

Give peace, O Lord, in all the world;
For only in you can we live in safety.
Lord, keep this nation under your care;
And guide us in the way of justice and truth.
Let your way be known upon earth;
Your saving health among all nations.
Let not the needy, O Lord, be forgotten;
Nor the hope of the poor be taken away.
Create in us clean hearts, O God;
And sustain us with your Holy Spirit.

Heavenly Father, in you we live and move and have
our being: We humbly pray you so to guide and
govern us by your Holy Spirit, that in all the cares and
occupations of our life we may not forget you, but may
remember that we are ever walking in your sight;
through Jesus Christ our Lord. **Amen.**

O God, you have made of one blood all the peoples of
the earth, and sent your blessed Son to preach peace to
those who are far off and to those who are near: Grant
that people everywhere may seek after you and find
you; bring the nations into your fold; pour out your
Spirit upon all flesh; and hasten the coming of your
kingdom; through Jesus Christ our Lord. **Amen.**

Prayer With Your Own Words

Almighty God, Father of all mercies, we your
unworthy servants give you humble thanks
for all your goodness and loving-kindness
to us and to all whom you have made.
**We bless you for our creation, preservation,
and all the blessings of this life;**

but above all for your immeasurable love
in the redemption of the world by our Lord Jesus
Christ; for the means of grace, and for the hope of
glory.
And, we pray,
give us such an awareness of your mercies,
that with truly thankful hearts
we may show forth your praise,
not only with our lips, but in our lives,
by giving our selves up to your service,
and by walking before you
in holiness and righteousness all our days;
through Jesus Christ our Lord,
to whom, with you and the Holy Spirit,
be honor and glory throughout all ages. **Amen.**
(The General Thanksgiving)

Let us bless the Lord.
Thanks be to God.

May the God of hope fill us with all joy and peace in
believing through the power of the Holy Spirit **Amen.**
(Romans 15:13)

Thursday
Midday Prayer

O God, make speed to save us.
O Lord, make haste to help us.

Midday Psalm

I lift up my eyes to the hills;
from where is my help to come?
My help comes from the Lord,
the maker of heaven and earth.
He will not let your foot be moved
and he who watches over you will not fall asleep.
Behold, he who keeps watch over Israel
shall neither slumber nor sleep;
The Lord himself watches over you;
the Lord is your shade at your right hand,
So that the sun shall not strike you by day,
nor the moon by night.
The Lord shall preserve you from all evil;
it is he who shall keep you safe.
The Lord shall watch over your going out
and your coming in,
from this time forth for evermore. (Psalm 121)

Glory to the Father, and to the Son, and to the Holy
Spirit: as it was in the beginning, is now, and will be
for ever. Amen.

Scripture Reading

If anyone is in Christ he is a new creation; the old has passed away, behold the new has come. All this is from God, who through Christ reconciled us to himself and gave us the ministry of reconciliation. (2 Corinthians 5:17-18)

Thanks be to God.

Prayer Without Words

Prayers of the People

Lord, have mercy.
Christ, have mercy.
Lord, have mercy.

The Lord's Prayer

Lord, hear our prayer;
And let our cry come to you.
Let us pray.

Heavenly Father, send your Holy Spirit into our hearts, to direct and rule us according to your will, to comfort us in all our afflictions, to defend us from all error, and to lead us into all truth; through Jesus Christ our Lord. **Amen.**

Prayer With Your Own Words

Let us bless the Lord.
Thanks be to God.

Thursday
Evening Prayer

I will bless the Lord who gives me counsel; my heart teaches me, night after night. I have set the Lord always before me; because he is at my right hand, I shall not fall. (Psalm 16:7-8)

O God, make speed to save us.
O Lord, make haste to help us.

Evening Psalm

I love the Lord, because he has heard
my voice and my supplications.
Because he inclined his ear to me,
therefore I will call on him as long as I live.
The snares of death encompassed me;
the pangs of Sheol laid hold on me;
I suffered distress and anguish.
Then I called on the name of the Lord:
"O Lord, I pray, save my life!"
Gracious is the Lord, and righteous;
our God is merciful.
The Lord protects the simple;
when I was brought low, he saved me.
Return, O my soul, to your rest,
for the Lord has dealt bountifully with you.
For you have delivered my soul from death,
my eyes from tears,
my feet from stumbling.
I walk before the Lord
in the land of the living.
I kept my faith, even when I said,

"I am greatly afflicted";
I said in my consternation,
"Everyone is a liar."
What shall I return to the Lord
for all his bounty to me?
I will lift up the cup of salvation
and call on the name of the Lord,
I will pay my vows to the Lord
in the presence of all his people.
Precious in the sight of the Lord
is the death of his faithful ones.
O Lord, I am your servant;
I am your servant, the child of your serving girl.
You have loosed my bonds.
I will offer to you a thanksgiving sacrifice
and call on the name of the Lord.
I will pay my vows to the Lord
in the presence of all his people,
in the courts of the house of the Lord,
in your midst, O Jerusalem.
Praise the Lord! (Psalm 116, NRSV)

Glory to the Father, and to the Son, and to the Holy Spirit: as it was in the beginning, is now, and will be for ever. Amen.

Scripture Reading
"Everyone then who hears these words of mine and acts on them will be like a wise man who built his house on rock. The rain fell, the floods came, and the winds blew and beat on that house, but it did not fall, because it had been founded on rock. And everyone who hears these words of mine and does not act on them will be like a foolish man who built his house on

158

sand. The rain fell, and the floods came, and the winds blew and beat against that house, and it fell—and great was its fall!" Now when Jesus had finished saying these things, the crowds were astounded at his teaching, for he taught them as one having authority, and not as their scribes. (Matthew 7:24-29, NRSV)

The Word of the Lord.
Thanks be to God.

Prayer Without Words

Response: The Song of Mary
   My soul proclaims the greatness of the Lord,
   my spirit rejoices in God my Savior;
   for he has looked with favor on his lowly servant.
   From this day all generations will call me blessed:
   the Almighty has done great things for me,
   and holy is his Name.
   He has mercy on those who fear him
   in every generation.
   He has shown the strength of his arm,
   he has scattered the proud in their conceit.
   He has cast down the mighty from their thrones,
   and has lifted up the lowly.
   He has filled the hungry with good things,
   and the rich he has sent away empty.
   He has come to the help of his servant Israel,
   for he has remembered his promise of mercy,
   The promise he made to our fathers,
   to Abraham and his children for ever. (Luke 1:46-55)

Prayers of the People
   The Lord be with us.
   Let us pray.

The Lord's Prayer

Show us your mercy, O Lord;
And grant us your salvation.
Clothe your ministers with righteousness;
Let your people sing with joy.
Give peace, O Lord, in all the world;
For only in you can we live in safety.
Lord, keep this nation under your care;
And guide us in the way of justice and truth.
Let your way be known upon earth;
Your saving health among all nations.
Let not the needy, O Lord, be forgotten;
Nor the hope of the poor be taken away.
Create in us clean hearts, O God;
And sustain us with your Holy Spirit.

Lord Jesus, stay with us, for evening is at hand and the day is past; be our companion in the way, kindle our hearts, and awaken hope, that we may know you as you are revealed in Scripture and the breaking of bread. Grant this for the sake of your love. **Amen.**

Keep watch, dear Lord, with those who work, or watch, or weep this night, and give your angels charge over those who sleep. Tend the sick, Lord Christ; give rest to the weary, bless the dying, soothe the suffering, pity the afflicted, shield the joyous; and all for your love's sake. **Amen.**

Hymn of the Day: Come, Sinners, to the Gospel Feast
(Charles Wesley)

Come, sinners, to the gospel feast;
let every soul be Jesus' guest.
Ye need not one be left behind,
for God hath bid all humankind.

Sent by my Lord, on you I call;
the invitation is to all.
Come, all the world! Come, sinner, thou!
All things in Christ are ready now.

Come, all ye souls by sin oppressed,
ye restless wanderers after rest;
ye poor, and maimed, and halt, and blind,
in Christ a hearty welcome find.

My message as from God receive;
ye all may come to Christ and live.
O let his love your hearts constrain,
nor suffer him to die in vain.

This is the time, no more delay!
This is the Lord's accepted day.
Come thou, this moment, at his call,
and live for him who died for all.

Prayer With Your Own Words

Almighty God, Father of all mercies, we your
unworthy servants give you humble thanks
for all your goodness and loving-kindness
to us and to all whom you have made.
**We bless you for our creation, preservation,
and all the blessings of this life;**

but above all for your immeasurable love
in the redemption of the world by our Lord Jesus
Christ; for the means of grace, and for the hope of
glory.
And, we pray,
give us such an awareness of your mercies,
that with truly thankful hearts
we may show forth your praise,
not only with our lips, but in our lives,
by giving our selves up to your service,
and by walking before you
in holiness and righteousness all our days;
through Jesus Christ our Lord,
to whom, with you and the Holy Spirit,
be honor and glory throughout all ages. **Amen.**
(The General Thanksgiving)

Let us bless the Lord.
Thanks be to God.

May the God of hope fill us with all joy and peace in
believing through the power of the Holy Spirit. **Amen.**
(Romans 15:13)

Thursday
Night Prayer

Call to Prayer

The Lord Almighty grant us a peaceful night and a perfect end. **Amen.**

Our help is in the Name of the Lord;
The maker of heaven and earth.

Confession

Let us confess our sins to God.

Silence

Almighty God, our heavenly Father:
We have sinned against you,
through our own fault,
in thought, and word, and deed,
and in what we have left undone.
For the sake of your Son our Lord Jesus Christ,
forgive us all our offenses;
and grant that we may serve you
in newness of life,
to the glory of your name. Amen.

May the Almighty God
grant us forgiveness of all our sins,
and the grace and comfort of the Holy Spirit. **Amen.**

O God, make speed to save us.
O Lord, make haste to help us.

Night Psalm

Answer me when I call, O God, defender of my cause;
you set me free when I am hard-pressed;
have mercy on me and hear my prayer.
"You mortals, how long will you dishonor my glory?
how long will you worship dumb idols
and run after false gods?"
Know that the Lord does wonders for the faithful;
when I call upon the Lord, he will hear me.
Tremble, then, and do not sin;
speak to your heart in silence upon your bed.
Offer the appointed sacrifices
and put your trust in the Lord.
Many are saying,
"Oh, that we might see better times!"
Lift up the light of your countenance upon us,
O Lord.
You have put gladness in my heart,
more than when grain and wine and oil increase.
I lie down in peace; at once I fall asleep;
for only you, Lord, make me dwell in safety. (Psalm 4)

Glory to the Father, and to the Son, and to the Holy
Spirit: as it was in the beginning, is now, and will be
for ever. Amen.

Scripture Reading

Lord, you are in the midst of us, and we are called by
your Name: Do not forsake us, O Lord our God.
(Jeremiah 14:9,22)

Thanks be to God.

Prayer Without Words

Prayers of the People
Into your hands, O Lord, I commend my spirit;
For you have redeemed me, O Lord, O God of truth.
Keep us, O Lord, as the apple of your eye;
Hide us under the shadow of your wings.

Lord, have mercy.
Christ, have mercy.
Lord, have mercy.

The Lord's Prayer

Lord, hear our prayer;
And let our cry come to you.
Let us pray.

Be our light in the darkness, O Lord, and in your great mercy defend us from all perils and dangers of this night; for the love of your only Son, our Savior Jesus Christ. **Amen.**

Keep watch, dear Lord, with those who work, or watch, or weep this night, and give your angels charge over those who sleep. Tend the sick, Lord Christ; give rest to the weary, bless the dying, soothe the suffering, pity the afflicted, shield the joyous; and all for your love's sake. **Amen.**

Prayer With Your Own Words

Benediction
Guide us waking, O Lord, and guard us sleeping; that awake we may watch with Christ, and asleep we may rest in peace.

The Song of Simeon
Lord, you now have set your servant free
to go in peace as you have promised;
For these eyes of mine have seen the Savior,
whom you have prepared for all the world to see:
A Light to enlighten the nations,
and the glory of your people Israel. (Luke 2:29-32)

Guide us waking, O Lord, and guard us sleeping; that
awake we may watch with Christ, and asleep we may
rest in peace.

Let us bless the Lord.
Thanks be to God.

The almighty and merciful Lord, Father, Son, and Holy
Spirit, bless us and keep us. **Amen.**

Friday
Morning Prayer

Call to Prayer

The hour is coming, and now is, when the true
worshipers will worship the Father in spirit and truth,
for such the Father seeks to worship him. (John 4:23)

Lord, open our lips.
And our mouth shall proclaim your praise.

The mercy of the Lord is everlasting:
Come let us adore him.

Psalm of Invitation

Be joyful in the Lord, all you lands;
serve the Lord with gladness
and come before his presence with a song.
Know this: the Lord himself is God;
he himself has made us, and we are his;
we are his people and the sheep of his pasture.
Enter his gates with thanksgiving;
go into his courts with praise;
give thanks to him and call upon his Name.
For the Lord is good;
his mercy is everlasting;
and his faithfulness endures from age to age.
(Psalm 100)

Morning Psalm

Have mercy on me, O God,
according to your steadfast love;
according to your abundant mercy
blot out my transgressions.
Wash me thoroughly from my iniquity,
and cleanse me from my sin.

For I know my transgressions,
and my sin is ever before me.
Against you, you alone, have I sinned,
and done what is evil in your sight,
so that you are justified in your sentence
and blameless when you pass judgment.
Indeed, I was born guilty,
a sinner when my mother conceived me.
You desire truth in the inward being;
therefore teach me wisdom in my secret heart.
Purge me with hyssop, and I shall be clean;
wash me, and I shall be whiter than snow.
Let me hear joy and gladness;
let the bones that you have crushed rejoice.
Hide your face from my sins,
and blot out all my iniquities.
Create in me a clean heart, O God,
and put a new and right spirit within me.
(Psalm 51:1-10 NRSV)

Glory to the Father, and to the Son, and to the Holy
Spirit: as it was in the beginning, is now, and will be
for ever. Amen.

Scripture Reading

I am the true vine, and my Father is the vinegrower. He
removes every branch in me that bears no fruit. Every
branch that bears fruit he prunes to make it bear more
fruit. You have already been cleansed by the word that
I have spoken to you. Abide in me as I abide in you.
Just as the branch cannot bear fruit by itself unless it
abides in the vine, neither can you unless you abide in
me. I am the vine, you are the branches. Those who
abide in me and I in them bear much fruit, because

apart from me you can do nothing. Whoever does not abide in me is thrown away like a branch and withers; such branches are gathered, thrown into the fire, and burned. If you abide in me, and my words abide in you, ask for whatever you wish, and it will be done for you. My Father is glorified by this, that you bear much fruit and become my disciples. (John 15:1-8, NRSV)

The Word of the Lord.
Thanks be to God.

Prayer Without Words

Response: A Song to the Lamb
Splendor and honor and kingly power
are yours by right, O Lord our God,
For you created everything that is,
and by your will they were created and have their being;
And yours by right, O Lamb that was slain,
for with your blood you have redeemed for God,
from every family, language, people, and nation, a
kingdom of priests to serve our God.
And so, to him who sits upon the throne,
and to Christ the Lamb, be worship and praise,
dominion and splendor, for ever and for evermore.
(Revelation 4:11, 5:9-10,13)

Prayers of the People
The Lord be with us.
Let us pray.

The Lord's Prayer

Save your people, Lord, and bless your inheritance;
Govern and uphold them, now and always.
Day by day we bless you;
We praise your Name for ever.
Lord, keep us from all sin today;
Have mercy on us, Lord, have mercy.
Lord, show us your love and mercy;
For we put our trust in you.
In you, Lord, is our hope;
And we shall never hope in vain.

Almighty God, whose most dear Son went not up to joy but first he suffered pain, and entered not into glory before he was crucified: Mercifully grant that we, walking in the way of the cross, may find it none other than the way of life and peace; through Jesus Christ your Son our Lord. **Amen.**

Lord Jesus Christ, you stretched out your arms of love on the hard wood of the cross that everyone might come within the reach of your saving embrace: So clothe us in your Spirit that we, reaching forth our hands in love, may bring those who do not know you to the knowledge and love of you; for the honor of your Name. **Amen.**

Prayer With Your Own Words

Almighty God, you have given us grace at this time with one accord to make our common supplication to you; and you have promised through your well-beloved Son that when two or three are gathered together in his Name you will be in the midst of them: Fulfill now, O Lord, our desires and petitions as may be best for us; granting us in this world knowledge of your truth, and in the age to come life everlasting. **Amen.** (A Prayer of St. Chrysostom)

Let us bless the Lord.
Thanks be to God.

Glory to God whose power, working in us, can do infinitely more than we can ask or imagine: Glory to him from generation to generation in the Church, and in Christ Jesus for ever and ever. **Amen.** (Ephesians 3:20-21)

Friday
Midday Prayer

O God, make speed to save us.
O Lord, make haste to help us.

Midday Psalm
When the Lord restored the fortunes of Zion,
then were we like those who dream.
Then was our mouth filled with laughter,
and our tongue with shouts of joy.
Then they said among the nations,
"The Lord has done great things for them."
The Lord has done great things for us,
and we are glad indeed.
Restore our fortunes, O Lord,
like the watercourses of the Negev.
Those who sowed with tears
will reap with songs of joy.
Those who go out weeping, carrying the seed,
will come again with joy, shouldering their sheaves.
(Psalm 126)

Glory to the Father, and to the Son, and to the Holy
Spirit: as it was in the beginning, is now, and will be
for ever. Amen.

Scripture Reading
From the rising of the sun to its setting my Name shall
be great among the nations, and in every place incense
shall be offered to my Name, and a pure offering; for
my Name shall be great among the nations, says the
Lord of Hosts. (Malachi 1:11)

Thanks be to God.

Prayer Without Words

Prayers of the People

Lord, have mercy.
Christ, have mercy.
Lord, have mercy.

The Lord's Prayer

Lord, hear our prayer;
And let our cry come to you.
Let us pray.

Blessed Savior, at this hour you hung upon the cross, stretching out your loving arms: Grant that all the peoples of the earth may look to you and be saved; for your tender mercies' sake. **Amen.**

Prayer With Your Own Words

Let us bless the Lord.
Thanks be to God.

Friday
Evening Prayer

Seek him who made the Pleiades and Orion, and turns deep darkness into morning, and darkens the day into night; who calls for the waters of the sea and pours them out upon the surface of the earth: The Lord is his name. (Amos 5:8)

O God, make speed to save us.
O Lord, make haste to help us.

Evening Psalm

My God, my God, why have you forsaken me? Why are you so far from helping me, from the words of my groaning?
O my God, I cry by day, but you do not answer; and by night, but find no rest.
Yet you are holy,
enthroned on the praises of Israel.
In you our ancestors trusted;
they trusted, and you delivered them.
To you they cried, and were saved;
in you they trusted, and were not put to shame.
But I am a worm, and not human;
scorned by others, and despised by the people.
All who see me mock at me;
they make mouths at me, they shake their heads;
"Commit your cause to the Lord; let him deliver— let him rescue the one in whom he delights!"

Yet it was you who took me from the womb;
you kept me safe on my mother's breast.
**On you I was cast from my birth, and since my
mother bore me you have been my God.**
Do not be far from me, for trouble is near and there is
no one to help. (Psalm 22:1-11, NRSV)

**Glory to the Father, and to the Son, and to the Holy
Spirit: as it was in the beginning, is now, and will be
for ever. Amen.**

Scripture Reading

For this reason I bow my knees before the Father, from
whom every family in heaven and on earth takes its
name. I pray that, according to the riches of his glory,
he may grant that you may be strengthened in your
inner being with power through his Spirit, and that
Christ may dwell in your hearts through faith, as you
are being rooted and grounded in love. I pray that you
may have the power to comprehend, with all the
saints, what is the breadth and length and height and
depth, and to know the love of Christ that surpasses
knowledge, so that you may be filled with all the
fullness of God. Now to him who by the power at work
within us is able to accomplish abundantly far more
than all we can ask or imagine, to him be glory in the
church and in Christ Jesus to all generations, forever
and ever. Amen. (Ephesians 3:14-21, NRSV)

The Word of the Lord.
Thanks be to God.

Prayer Without Words

Response: The Song of Simeon
Lord, you now have set your servant free
to go in peace as you have promised;
For these eyes of mine have seen the Savior,
whom you have prepared for all the world to see:
A Light to enlighten the nations,
and the glory of your people Israel. (Luke 2:29-32)

Prayers of the People
The Lord be with us.
Let us pray.

The Lord's Prayer

That this evening may be holy, good, and peaceful,
we entreat you, O Lord.
That your holy angels may lead us in paths of peace
and goodwill, **we entreat you, O Lord.**
That we may be pardoned and forgiven for our sins
and offenses, **we entreat you, O Lord.**
That there may be peace to your Church and to the
whole world, **we entreat you, O Lord.**
That we may depart this life in your faith and fear, and
not be condemned before the great judgment seat of
Christ, **we entreat you, O Lord.**
That we may be bound together by your Holy Spirit in
the communion of [_____ and] all your saints,
entrusting one another and all our life to Christ,
we entreat you, O Lord.

Lord Jesus Christ, by your death you took away the
sting of death: Grant to us your servants so to follow in
faith where you have led the way, that we may at
length fall asleep peacefully in you and wake up in
your likeness; for your tender mercies' sake. **Amen.**

O God, you manifest in your servants the signs of your presence: Send forth upon us the Spirit of love, that in companionship with one another your abounding grace may increase among us; through Jesus Christ our Lord. **Amen.**

Hymn of the Day: *O Love Divine, What Hast Thou Done* (*Charles Wesley*)

O Love divine, what has thou done!
The immortal God hath died for me!
The Father's coeternal Son
bore all my sins upon the tree.
Th' immortal God for me hath died:
My Lord, my Love, is crucified!

Is crucified for me and you,
to bring us rebels back to God.
Believe, believe the record true,
ye all are bought with Jesus' blood.
Pardon for all flows from his side:
My Lord, my Love, is crucified!

Behold him, all ye that pass by,
the bleeding Prince of life and peace!
Come, sinners, see your Savior die,
and say, "Was ever grief like his?"
Come, feel with me his blood applied:
My Lord, my Love, is crucified!

Prayer With Your Own Words

Almighty God, you have given us grace at this time with one accord to make our common supplication to you; and you have promised through your well-beloved Son that when two or three are gathered together in his Name you will be in the midst of them: Fulfill now, O Lord, our desires and petitions as may be best for us; granting us in this world knowledge of your truth, and in the age to come life everlasting. **Amen.** (A Prayer of St. Chrysostom)

Let us bless the Lord.
Thanks be to God.

Glory to God whose power, working in us, can do infinitely more than we can ask or imagine: Glory to him from generation to generation in the Church, and in Christ Jesus for ever and ever. **Amen.** (Ephesians 3:20-21)

Friday
Night Prayer

Call to Prayer

The Lord Almighty grant us a peaceful night and a perfect end. **Amen.**

Our help is in the Name of the Lord;
The maker of heaven and earth.

Confession

Let us confess our sins to God.

Silence

Almighty God, our heavenly Father:
We have sinned against you,
through our own fault,
in thought, and word, and deed,
and in what we have left undone.
For the sake of your Son our Lord Jesus Christ,
forgive us all our offenses;
and grant that we may serve you
in newness of life,
to the glory of your name. Amen.

May the Almighty God
grant us forgiveness of all our sins,
and the grace and comfort of the Holy Spirit. **Amen.**

O God, make speed to save us.
O Lord, make haste to help us.

Night Psalm

In you, O Lord, have I taken refuge;
let me never be put to shame:
deliver me in your righteousness.
Incline your ear to me;
make haste to deliver me.
Be my strong rock, a castle to keep me safe,
for you are my crag and my stronghold;
for the sake of your Name, lead me and guide me.
Take me out of the net that they have secretly set for
me,
for you are my tower of strength.
Into your hands I commend my spirit,
for you have redeemed me,
O Lord, O God of truth. (Psalm 31)

Glory to the Father, and to the Son, and to the Holy
Spirit: as it was in the beginning, is now, and will be
for ever. Amen.

Scripture Reading

Come to me, all who labor and are heavy-laden, and I
will give you rest. Take my yoke upon you, and learn
from me; for I am gentle and lowly in heart, and you
will find rest for your souls. For my yoke is easy, and
my burden is light. (Matthew 11:28-30)

Thanks be to God.

Prayer Without Words

Prayers of the People

Into your hands, O Lord, I commend my spirit;
For you have redeemed me, O Lord, O God of truth.
Keep us, O Lord, as the apple of your eye;
Hide us under the shadow of your wings.

Lord, have mercy.
Christ, have mercy.
Lord, have mercy.

The Lord's Prayer

Lord, hear our prayer;
And let our cry come to you.
Let us pray.

Be present, O merciful God, and protect us through the hours of this night, so that we who are wearied by the changes and chances of this life may rest in your eternal changelessness; through Jesus Christ our Lord. **Amen.**

O God, your unfailing providence sustains both the world we live in and the life we live: Watch over those, both night and day, who work while others sleep, and grant that we may never forget that our common life depends upon each other's toil; through Jesus Christ our Lord. **Amen.**

Prayer With Your Own Words

Benediction

Guide us waking, O Lord, and guard us sleeping; that awake we may watch with Christ, and asleep we may rest in peace.

The Song of Simeon
Lord, you now have set your servant free
to go in peace as you have promised;
For these eyes of mine have seen the Savior,
whom you have prepared for all the world to see:
A Light to enlighten the nations,
and the glory of your people Israel. (Luke 2:29-32)

Guide us waking, O Lord, and guard us sleeping; that awake we may watch with Christ, and asleep we may rest in peace.

Let us bless the Lord.
Thanks be to God.

The almighty and merciful Lord, Father, Son, and Holy Spirit, bless us and keep us. **Amen.**

Saturday
Morning Prayer

<u>*Call to Prayer*</u>

Thus says the high and lofty One who inhabits eternity, whose name is Holy, "I dwell in the high and holy place and also with the one who has a contrite and humble spirit, to revive the spirit of the humble and to revive the heart of the contrite." (Isaiah 57:15)

Lord, open our lips.
And our mouth shall proclaim your praise.

The earth is the Lord's for he made it:
Come let us adore him.

<u>*Psalm of Invitation*</u>

Come, let us sing to the Lord.
Let us shout for joy to the Rock of our salvation.
Let us come before his presence with thanksgiving
and raise a loud shout to him with psalms.
For the Lord is a great God,
and a great King above all gods.
In his hand are the caverns of the earth,
and the heights of the hills are his also.
The sea is his, for he made it,
and his hands have molded the dry land.
Come, let us bow down, and bend the knee,
and kneel before the Lord our Maker.
For he is our God,
and we are the people of his pasture
and the sheep of his hand.
Oh, that today you would hearken to his voice!
(Psalm 95:1-7)

Morning Psalm

The Lord is my shepherd, I shall not want.
He makes me lie down in green pastures;
he leads me beside still waters;
he restores my soul.
He leads me in right paths for his name's sake.
Even though I walk through the darkest valley,
I fear no evil;
for you are with me; your rod and your staff—
they comfort me.
You prepare a table before me
in the presence of my enemies;
you anoint my head with oil; my cup overflows.
Surely goodness and mercy shall follow me
all the days of my life,
and I shall dwell in the house of the Lord
my whole life long. (Psalm 23, NRSV)

Glory to the Father, and to the Son, and to the Holy
Spirit: as it was in the beginning, is now, and will be
for ever. Amen.

Scripture Reading

But now thus says the Lord, he who created you, O
Jacob, he who formed you, O Israel: Do not fear, for I
have redeemed you; I have called you by name, you
are mine. When you pass through the waters, I will be
with you; and through the rivers, they shall not
overwhelm you; when you walk through fire you shall
not be burned, and the flame shall not consume you.
For I am the Lord your God, the Holy One of Israel,
your Savior. (Isaiah 43:1-3a, NRSV)

The Word of the Lord.
Thanks be to God.

Prayer Without Words

Response: *The Song of the Redeemed*
O ruler of the universe, Lord God,
great deeds are they that you have done,
surpassing human understanding.
Your ways are ways of righteousness and truth,
O King of all the ages.
Who can fail to do you homage, Lord,
and sing the praises of your Name?
For you only are the Holy One.
All nations will draw near
and fall down before you,
because your just and holy works
have been revealed. (Revelation 15:3-4)

Prayers of the People
The Lord be with us.
Let us pray.

The Lord's Prayer

Show us your mercy, O Lord;
And grant us your salvation.
Clothe your ministers with righteousness;
Let your people sing with joy.
Give peace, O Lord, in all the world;
For only in you can we live in safety.
Lord, keep this nation under your care;
And guide us in the way of justice and truth.
Let your way be known upon earth;
Your saving health among all nations.

Let not the needy, O Lord, be forgotten;
Nor the hope of the poor be taken away.
Create in us clean hearts, O God;
And sustain us with your Holy Spirit.

Almighty God, who after the creation of the world
rested from all your works and sanctified a day of rest
for all your creatures: Grant that we, putting away all
earthly anxieties, may be duly prepared for the service
of your sanctuary, and that our rest here upon earth
may be a preparation for the eternal rest promised to
your people in heaven; through Jesus Christ our Lord.
Amen.

Almighty and everlasting God, by whose Spirit the
whole body of your faithful people is governed and
sanctified: Receive our supplications and prayers
which we offer before you for all members of your holy
Church, that in their vocation and ministry they may
truly and devoutly serve you; through our Lord Jesus
Christ. **Amen.**

Prayer With Your Own Words

Almighty God, Father of all mercies, we your
unworthy servants give you humble thanks
for all your goodness and loving-kindness
to us and to all whom you have made.
We bless you for our creation, preservation,
and all the blessings of this life;
but above all for your immeasurable love
in the redemption of the world by our Lord Jesus
Christ; for the means of grace, and for the hope of
glory.

And, we pray,
give us such an awareness of your mercies,
that with truly thankful hearts
we may show forth your praise,
not only with our lips, but in our lives,
by giving our selves up to your service,
and by walking before you
in holiness and righteousness all our days;
through Jesus Christ our Lord,
to whom, with you and the Holy Spirit,
be honor and glory throughout all ages. **Amen.**
(The General Thanksgiving)

Let us bless the Lord.
Thanks be to God.

The grace of our Lord Jesus Christ, and the love of God,
and the fellowship of the Holy Spirit, be with us all
evermore. **Amen.** (2 Corinthians 13:14)

Saturday
Midday Prayer

O God, make speed to save us.
O Lord, make haste to help us.

Midday Psalm
Your word is a lantern to my feet
and a light upon my path.
I have sworn and am determined
to keep your righteous judgments.
I am deeply troubled;
preserve my life, O Lord, according to your word.
Accept, O Lord, the willing tribute of my lips,
and teach me your judgments.
My life is always in my hand,
yet I do not forget your law.
The wicked have set a trap for me,
but I have not strayed from your commandments.
Your decrees are my inheritance for ever;
truly, they are the joy of my heart.
I have applied my heart to fulfill your statutes
for ever and to the end. (Psalm 119:105-112)

Glory to the Father, and to the Son, and to the Holy
Spirit: as it was in the beginning, is now, and will be
for ever. Amen.

Scripture Reading
The love of God has been poured into our hearts
through the Holy Spirit that has been given to us.
(Romans 5:5)

Thanks be to God.

Prayer Without Words

Prayers of the People
Lord, have mercy.
Christ, have mercy.
Lord, have mercy.

The Lord's Prayer

Lord, hear our prayer;
And let our cry come to you.
Let us pray.

Almighty Savior, who at noonday called your servant Saint Paul to be an apostle to the Gentiles: We pray you to illumine the world with the radiance of your glory, that all nations may come and worship you; for you live and reign for ever and ever. **Amen.**

Prayer With Your Own Words

Let us bless the Lord.
Thanks be to God.

Saturday
Evening Prayer

Call to Prayer

If I say, "Surely the darkness will cover me, and the light around me turn to night," darkness is not dark to you, O Lord; the night is as bright as the day; darkness and light to you are both alike. (Psalm 139:10-11)

O God, make speed to save us.
O Lord, make haste to help us.

Evening Psalm

Unless the Lord builds the house,
those who build it labor in vain.
Unless the Lord guards the city,
the guard keeps watch in vain.
It is in vain that you rise up early
and go late to rest,
eating the bread of anxious toil;
for he gives sleep to his beloved.
(Psalm 127:1-2, NRSV)

Glory to the Father, and to the Son, and to the Holy Spirit: as it was in the beginning, is now, and will be for ever. Amen.

Scripture Reading

As the Father has loved me, so I have loved you; abide in my love. If you keep my commandments, you will abide in my love, just as I have kept my Father's commandments and abide in his love. I have said these things to you so that my joy may be in you, and that your joy may be complete.

This is my commandment, that you love one another as I have loved you. No one has greater love than this, to lay down one's life for one's friends. You are my friends if you do what I command you. I do not call you servants any longer, because the servant does not know what the master is doing; but I have called you friends, because I have made known to you everything that I have heard from my Father. You did not choose me but I chose you. And I appointed you to go and bear fruit, fruit that will last, so that the Father will give you whatever you ask him in my name. I am giving you these commands so that you may love one another. (John 15:9-17, NRSV)

The Word of the Lord.

Thanks be to God.

Prayer Without Words

Response: The Song of Mary

My soul proclaims the greatness of the Lord,
my spirit rejoices in God my Savior;
for he has looked with favor on his lowly servant.
From this day all generations will call me blessed:
the Almighty has done great things for me,
and holy is his Name.
He has mercy on those who fear him
in every generation.
He has shown the strength of his arm,
he has scattered the proud in their conceit.
He has cast down the mighty from their thrones,
and has lifted up the lowly.
He has filled the hungry with good things,
and the rich he has sent away empty.

He has come to the help of his servant Israel,
for he has remembered his promise of mercy,
The promise he made to our fathers,
to Abraham and his children for ever. (Luke 1:46-55)

Prayers of the People

The Lord be with us.
Let us pray.

The Lord's Prayer

Show us your mercy, O Lord;
And grant us your salvation.
Clothe your ministers with righteousness;
Let your people sing with joy.
Give peace, O Lord, in all the world;
For only in you can we live in safety.
Lord, keep this nation under your care;
And guide us in the way of justice and truth.
Let your way be known upon earth;
Your saving health among all nations.
Let not the needy, O Lord, be forgotten;
Nor the hope of the poor be taken away.
Create in us clean hearts, O God;
And sustain us with your Holy Spirit.

O God, the source of eternal light: Shed forth your
unending day upon us who watch for you, that our
lips may praise you, our lives may bless you, and our
worship on the morrow give you glory; through Jesus
Christ our Lord. **Amen.**

O God and Father of all, whom the whole heavens adore: Let the whole earth also worship you, all nations obey you, all tongues confess and bless you, and men and women everywhere love you and serve you in peace; through Jesus Christ our Lord. **Amen.**

Hymn of the Day: Love Divine, All Loves Excelling |
(Charles Wesley)
    Love divine, all loves excelling,
    joy of heaven, to earth come down;
    fix in us thy humble dwelling;
    all thy faithful mercies crown!
    Jesus thou art all compassion,
    pure, unbounded love thou art;
    visit us with thy salvation;
    enter every trembling heart.

    Breathe, O breathe thy loving Spirit
    into every troubled breast!
    Let us all in thee inherit;
    let us find that second rest.
    Take away our bent to sinning;
    Alpha and Omega be;
    end of faith, as its beginning,
    set our hearts at liberty.

    Come, Almighty to deliver,
    let us all thy life receive;
    suddenly return and never,
    nevermore thy temples leave.
    Thee we would be always blessing,
    serve thee as thy hosts above,
    pray and praise thee without ceasing,
    glory in thy perfect love.

Finish, then, thy new creation;
pure and spotless let us be.
Let us see thy great salvation
perfectly restored in thee;
changed from glory into glory,
till in heaven we take our place,
till we cast our crowns before thee,
lost in wonder, love, and praise.

Prayer With Your Own Words

Almighty God, Father of all mercies, we your
unworthy servants give you humble thanks
for all your goodness and loving-kindness
to us and to all whom you have made.
**We bless you for our creation, preservation,
and all the blessings of this life;**
but above all for your immeasurable love
in the redemption of the world by our Lord Jesus
Christ; for the means of grace, and for the hope of
glory.
**And, we pray,
give us such an awareness of your mercies,
that with truly thankful hearts
we may show forth your praise,
not only with our lips, but in our lives,
by giving our selves up to your service,
and by walking before you
in holiness and righteousness all our days;**
through Jesus Christ our Lord,
to whom, with you and the Holy Spirit,
be honor and glory throughout all ages. **Amen.**
(The General Thanksgiving)

Let us bless the Lord.
Thanks be to God.

The grace of our Lord Jesus Christ, and the love of God, and the fellowship of the Holy Spirit, be with us all evermore. **Amen.** (2 Corinthians 13:14)

Saturday
Night Prayer

Call to Prayer

The Lord Almighty grant us a peaceful night and a perfect end. **Amen.**

Our help is in the Name of the Lord;
The maker of heaven and earth.

Confession

Let us confess our sins to God.

Silence

Almighty God, our heavenly Father:
We have sinned against you,
through our own fault,
in thought, and word, and deed,
and in what we have left undone.
For the sake of your Son our Lord Jesus Christ,
forgive us all our offenses;
and grant that we may serve you
in newness of life,
to the glory of your name. Amen.

May the Almighty God
grant us forgiveness of all our sins,
and the grace and comfort of the Holy Spirit. **Amen.**

O God, make speed to save us.
O Lord, make haste to help us.

Night Psalm

He who dwells in the shelter of the Most High
abides under the shadow of the Almighty.
He shall say to the Lord,
"You are my refuge and my stronghold,
my God in whom I put my trust."
He shall deliver you from the snare of the hunter
and from the deadly pestilence.
He shall cover you with his pinions,
and you shall find refuge under his wings;
his faithfulness shall be a shield and a buckler.
You shall not be afraid of any terror by night,
nor of the arrow that flies by day;
Of the plague that stalks in the darkness,
nor of the sickness that lays waste at mid-day.
A thousand shall fall at your side
and ten thousand at your right hand,
but it shall not come near you.
Your eyes have only to behold
to see the reward of the wicked.
Because you have made the Lord your refuge,
and the Most High your habitation,
There shall no evil happen to you,
neither shall any plague come near your dwelling.
For he shall give his angels charge over you,
to keep you in all your ways.
They shall bear you in their hands,
lest you dash your foot against a stone.
You shall tread upon the lion and the adder;
you shall trample the young lion and the serpent
under your feet.
Because he is bound to me in love,
therefore will I deliver him;

I will protect him, because he knows my Name.
He shall call upon me, and I will answer him;
I am with him in trouble;
I will rescue him and bring him to honor.
With long life will I satisfy him,
and show him my salvation. (Psalm 91)

Glory to the Father, and to the Son, and to the Holy
Spirit: as it was in the beginning, is now, and will be
for ever. Amen.

Scripture Reading
May the God of peace, who brought again from the
dead our Lord Jesus, the great shepherd of the sheep,
by the blood of the eternal covenant, equip you with
everything good that you may do his will, working in
you that which is pleasing in his sight; through Jesus
Christ, to whom be glory for ever and ever.
(Hebrews 13:20-21)

Thanks be to God.

Prayer Without Words

Prayers of the People
Into your hands, O Lord, I commend my spirit;
For you have redeemed me, O Lord, O God of truth.
Keep us, O Lord, as the apple of your eye;
Hide us under the shadow of your wings.

Lord, have mercy.
Christ, have mercy.
Lord, have mercy.

The Lord's Prayer

Lord, hear our prayer;
And let our cry come to you.
Let us pray.

We give you thanks, O God, for revealing your Son
Jesus Christ to us by the light of his resurrection: Grant
that as we sing your glory at the close of this day, our
joy may abound in the morning as we celebrate the
Paschal mystery; through Jesus Christ our Lord. **Amen.**

Keep watch, dear Lord, with those who work, or
watch, or weep this night, and give your angels charge
over those who sleep. Tend the sick, Lord Christ; give
rest to the weary, bless the dying, soothe the suffering,
pity the afflicted, shield the joyous; and all for your
love's sake. **Amen.**

Prayer With Your Own Words

Benediction
**Guide us waking, O Lord, and guard us sleeping; that
awake we may watch with Christ, and asleep we may
rest in peace.**

The Song of Simeon
Lord, you now have set your servant free
to go in peace as you have promised;
**For these eyes of mine have seen the Savior,
whom you have prepared for all the world to see:**
A Light to enlighten the nations,
and the glory of your people Israel. (Luke 2:29-32)

**Guide us waking, O Lord, and guard us sleeping; that
awake we may watch with Christ, and asleep we may
rest in peace.**

Let us bless the Lord.
Thanks be to God.

The almighty and merciful Lord, Father, Son, and Holy Spirit, bless us and keep us. **Amen.**

A Note to Pastors and Ministry Leaders

In each place where I have been involved in ministry, there have been good people who have sincerely desired to grow in their lives with God. I am certain that you encounter these people in your ministries as well. My greatest hope for this book is that it would prove helpful to them. Because of this, I would like to invite you to consider the following three opportunities:

Create a Special Edition of *Live Prayerfully* specifically for your church or organization.

If you think it would be helpful for this book to become a go-to resource for people within your church or ministry in their efforts to learn to pray, print-on-demand technology allows us to customize the book for your needs. You can write an additional foreword for the book, as well as listing "Special Edition for [Your Church Name]" on the cover. Any number of copies you choose (from 1 to 1 million!) can be made available to your ministry at a discounted price. To explore this option, visit www.salvationlife.com or email me at daniel@salvationlife.com.

Bring a *Live Prayerfully* retreat to your church.

At www.salvationlife.com, you can find a sample schedule for one or two-night retreats based on this book. The retreats are designed to be restful, helpful, and enjoyable.

Consider joining a *Transforming Community*.

As a ministry leader, if you find the things in this book helpful, it is natural for you to think of ways that it might also be helpful to others, which the two items on the previous page address. While that isn't bad, there's still a better option: you can learn to live prayerfully, and then your prayerful living will inevitably affect those around you. The best way I know to encourage this in Christian leaders is by participation in a *Transforming Community*.

I participated in one from 2009-2011, and the experience was invaluable, as it gave me the permission and support which I had so long felt I needed to arrange my life around my desire for God.

The *Transforming Community* is a group of pastors and Christian leaders who commit themselves to quarterly retreats over a two year time period for the purpose of experiencing deeper levels of spiritual transformation. As part of the ministry of the Transforming Center, led by Ruth Haley Barton, you will find excellent teaching, guidance in practices that will nourish your soul, and a wonderfully supportive group of like-minded leaders.

For more information, see the Transforming Center's website at www.transformingcenter.org, or my post, "How the Transforming Community Saved My Life" at www.salvationlife.com/transforming-community/.

Gratitudes

Having never attempted to write a real book prior to this one, I never realized how many people need to be involved in different ways to make it happen. These are some of them, to each of whom I am deeply grateful:

I would have never had the courage to develop the class, which turned into the retreat, which turned into this book, if it had not been for spiritual direction sessions with Sibyl Towner during my Transforming Community experience. Ruth Haley Barton and the entire Transforming Community were of tremendous encouragement and support to me during a period when I desperately needed it.

As I began to work this project into a book format, I sought and received feedback from a fairly large group of people. Alayna Brooks, Kendon Wheeler, Laura Laffoon, Steve Pitts, and Ryan Bash each offered very helpful feedback. Then also the entire group of folks who made comments on the related posts on my blog helped keep me motivated to get this finished. Christy Swaringen particularly went beyond the call of duty, which doesn't surprise anyone who knows her.

Thanks to Jason Stevens for helping me out in getting the various covers just right. He has been my tutor in all things Mac for about 15 years now, since we were roommates throughout my college years.

Perhaps the most pleasant surprise from this process was discovering Emily Bosland's skills as an editor. She helped me make the project better, and it was a delight to work with her on it.

I deeply needed to hear the way that Wil Hernandez communicated his belief in this project and my pursuit of it. I leave every conversation with him encouraged, and his friendship and guidance are important graces to me.

The book, as well as the classes and retreats that led to it, would have never come about as they have without Tim Walker. He has provided wonderful opportunities for me, including the generous space to discern the way in which I can best be of service to God's kingdom.

Robert Pelfrey has been an encouraging friend through every step of this project. He's been at the classes and retreats, has allowed me to bounce countless ideas off of his wonderful brain, and has been a true friend, encouraging me every step of the way.

Family matters tremendously in something like this. My mom, Cathy Harris, has been the person I've known the longest who has consistently modeled for me the desire to live prayerfully. I hope that this book is a partial reflection of her investment in me. So also with my in-laws, Tim and Linda Holeman. Their editing, encouragement, meals, and a basement to write in are all invaluable.

Ethan and Mia don't realize that they're contributing anything to their dad's first attempt at a book, but perhaps my greatest motivation to live prayerfully is so that I can love and parent them well. They are my treasures.

Finally, my wife, Kara, is simply the best. I would be a mess without her. She has not only believed in me doing this kind of thing from the beginning and helped to make it possible in numerous ways, but second only to God, is the one most responsible for helping me become the kind of person who might have something worth saying. I love her like crazy.

Notes

[1] Albert Haase, *Coming Home to Your True Self: Leaving the Emptiness of False Attractions* (Downers Grove, Ill.: InterVarsity Press, 2008), p. 84. Kindle Edition.

[2] N.T. Wright, *The Lord and His Prayer* (Grand Rapids, Mich.: Wm. B. Eerdmans Publishing, 1997), p. 2.

[3] Scot McKnight, *Praying With the Church: Following Jesus Daily, Hourly, Today* (Brewster, Mass.: Paraclete Press, 2006), p. 4.

[4] See Steve Harper, *Devotional Life in the Wesleyan Tradition: A Workbook* (Nashville, Tenn.: Upper Room Books, 1995) pp. 45-58.

[5] McKnight, *Praying With the Church*, pp. 5-6.

[6] See Psalm 8:2 and Matthew 21:16

[7] See Psalm 118:22-23 and Matthew 21:42

[8] See Psalm 118:26 and Matthew 23:39

[9] See Psalm 22:1 and Matthew 27:46

[10] James Bryan Smith, *The Good and Beautiful God: Falling in Love With the God Jesus Knows* (Downers Grove, Ill.: InterVarsity Press, 2009), p. 91.

[11] From an article on the Anglican office of Morning Prayer, accessed November 12, 2012, http://www.tititudorancea.org/z/morning_prayer.htm.

[12] Robert Benson, *In Constant Prayer* (Nashville, Tenn.: Thomas Nelson, 2008) pp. 62-63.

[13] Ibid., p. 66.

[14] John of the Cross, *The Dark Night of the Soul*, as quoted in *Devotional Classics: Selected Readings for Indivituals and Groups*, ed. Richard J. Foster and James Bryan Smith (San Francisco: HarperSanFrancisco, 1993), p. 36.

[15] Ruth Haley Barton, *Invitation to Solitude and Silence: Experiencing God's Transforming Presence* (Downers Grove, Ill.: InterVarsity Press, 2004), p. 21.

[16] Ibid., p. 20.

[17] Thomas Merton, *Contemplative Prayer* (New York: Crown Publishing Group, 1996), pp. 10-11.

[18] Brennan Manning, *The Signature of Jesus* (Colorado Springs: Multnomah Books, 1996), p. 205.

[19] Dallas Willard, *The Spirit of the Disciplines: Understanding How God Changes Lives* (New York: HarperCollins, 1988), p.163.

[20] Haase, *Coming Home to Your True Self*, pp. 88-89.

[21] *Nooma: Noise*. DVD. Rob Bell Grand Rapids, Mich.: Zondervan, 2005.

[22] Richard J. Foster, *Prayer: Finding the Heart's True Home* (New York: HarperCollins, 1992), p. 14.

[23] Henri J.M. Nouwen, *The Way of the Heart: Desert Spirituality and Contemporary Ministry* (San Francisco: HarperCollins, 1981), p. 27.

[24] Thomas Keating, *Open Mind, Open Heart* (New York: Continuum, 2009), p. 49.

[25] M. Basil Pennington, *Centering Prayer* (New York: Doubleday, 1980), pp. 68-69.

[26] N.T. Wright, *The Early Christian Letters for Everyone: James, Peter, John, and Judah* (Louisville: Westminster John Knox Press, 2011), p. 29.

[27] Norman Harrison, *His in a Life of Prayer*, as quoted in Glenn Clark, *I Will Lift Up Mine Eyes* (Harper & Rowe Publishers, 1937), as quoted in Rueben P. Job and Norman Shawchuck, *A Guide to Prayer for Ministers and Other Servants*, (Nashville: The Upper Room, 1983), p. 293.

[28] Dallas Willard, *The Divine Conspiracy: Rediscovering Our Hidden Life in God* (New York: HarperOne, 1997), p. 243.

[29] Richard J. Foster, *Prayer: Finding the Heart's True Home* (New York: HarperCollins, 1992) p. 9.

[30] Ibid., p. 10.

[31] Ibid., p. 11.

[32] Ibid., p. 13.

[33] See Chapter Five of Mark Gungor, *Laugh Your Way to a Better Marriage* (New York: Simon & Schuster, 2008).

[34] Dallas Willard, *Hearing God: Developing a Conversational Relationship with God* (Downers Grove, Ill.: InterVarsity Press, 1999) pp. 163-165.

[35] A classic method for reading the scriptures in this way is called *lectio divina*. For a helpful guide in this practice, see Richard Peace, *Contemplative Bible Reading: Experiencing God Through Scripture.*

[36] Benson, *In Constant Prayer*, p. 119.

[37] In this sense, "catholic" means "universal," rather than referring specifically to the Roman Catholic Church.